John Alexander Wilson

Sketches of Ancient Maori Life and History

John Alexander Wilson

Sketches of Ancient Maori Life and History

ISBN/EAN: 9783337330972

Printed in Europe, USA, Canada, Australia, Japan

Cover: Foto ©Thomas Meinert / pixelio.de

More available books at **www.hansebooks.com**

✳ SKETCHES ✳

....OF....

Ancient Maori Life & History

JOHN ALEXANDER WILSON

LATELY A JUDGE OF THE NATIVE LAND COURT OF NEW ZEALAND, AUTHOR
OF "STORY OF TE WAHAROA."

REPRINTED FROM THE "AUCKLAND STAR."

Price 2/6

Auckland:

H. BRETT, PRINTER, STAR AND GRAPHIC OFFICE, SHORTLAND STREET.
CHAMPTALOUP & COOPER, PUBLISHERS, QUEEN STREET.

1894.

ERRATA.

On page 7, first column, on line 14 from bottom, *for* Ngaterna *read* Ngatirna.

On page 8, second column, on line 31 from bottom, *for* Whangaroa, where he, *read* Whangara, where she.

On same page and column, on line 18 from bottom, *for* Prengatoetoe *read* Paengatoetoe.

SKETCHES

OF

ANCIENT MAORI LIFE AND HISTORY

BY

JOHN ALEXANDER WILSON,

LATELY A JUDGE OF THE NATIVE LAND COURT OF NEW ZEALAND; AUTHOR OF
"STORY OF TE WAHAROA."

THE MAUI MAORI NATION.

I VENTURE, with the permission of the reader, to offer a few remarks upon some portions of the early history of the Maori race. Statements in various forms are constantly being made public, many of them more or less erroneous, and more or less important according to the sources whence promulgated ; and it is to remove the misapprehension that gives rise to such statements, that I would mention some points that have escaped general observation.

My informants are mostly deceased, and if asked for authorities I regret to say that in the majority of cases I can only point to ' Where heaves the turf in many a mouldering heap.' These remarks are, however, based upon inquiries made by myself and by my father, the Rev. J. A. Wilson, before me, and extend back sixty years from the present time (1894).

I will begin by introducing an ancient Maori tradition at which a descendant of Noah cannot afford to smile, unless he is prepared to claim for his own ancestor, and ;or the northern hemisphere, a monopoly of diluvian adventure.

The tradition says there was a time when the waters covered the earth : that, at that time, Maui and his three sons floated upon the waters in a canoe, fishing ; that presently Maui hooked the earth, and with great labour he drew it to the surface with the assistance of his sons. Then their canoe grounded upon what proved to be the top of a mountain. As the earth became bare the sons of Maui took possession ; but Maui himself vanished and returned to the place from whence he came. The canoe remained upon the top of the mountain, where it may be seen in a petrified state ; that present time. Hikurangi Mountain, at the head of Waiapu Valley, is this southern Ararat whence the descendants of Maui peopled the North Island of New Zealand. They named their island Te Ika a Maui (Maui's fish), or Ehinomaui (fished up by Maui). The head of the fish is at Cook's Strait and the tail at the North Cape, where there is a subterranean opening by the seashore through which departed spirits pass to the lower regions, when they leave this World of Light (Aomarama). From this it will be seen that the ancient descendants of Maui had a good geographical knowledge of the shape of their island. I should add that the hills and valleys on the surface of the island were made by the occupants of the canoe getting out and tramping on the soil while wet and in a muddy state, thus making hills and holes. Omitting much circumlocutory description is the story of how Maui fished up the North Island of New Zealand as it was told fifty years ago by the natives. Since that time, I observe that some of them have changed Maui's sons into his brothers.

In course of time the people of Maui increased and spread themselves in tribes and hapus over the greater portion of the island. Probably they occupied the whole of it, but this I cannot affirm. It seems, however, to be clear that at the time when the canoes of immigrants came from Hawaiki, about six hundred years ago, that the Maui or Maori nation inhabited the country from Wairarapa in the south to Waitakere north of Auckland, and from Tuparoa and Hicks' Bay in the east to the neighbourhood of Mokan and Kawhia in the west.

The aborigines did not cultivate the soil for food—excepting the hue gourd, from which calabashes were made ; they had no useful plants that they could cultivate. They ate berries and the shoots and roots of ferns and other plants, as they found them growing wild in the forests, and in the open country. For flesh they hunted the moa,[*] and caught the kakapo‡ at night, and they snared pigeons, kakas, and many other kinds of birds. They fished with the seine and line in salt water and fresh. They dived from the rocks for crayfish, and in the swamps they caught eels. Before the advent of the Hawaikians they had neither taro nor kumara, nor karaka berries, they were unable to make kao,‡ and they had no rats.§ They stored their food in chambers called ruas, hollowed out of the ground where the soil was dry. They cooked their food in the Maori umu, just as they do now. Their clothing was made from flax, for the aute tree, whence tappa cloth is made, had not yet been introduced from Hawaiki. They spoke the Maori language. Their population was mostly distributed, not necessarily where the land was fertile, but where the forests were rich in birds, as at Motu; where streams and swamps yielded fish and eels plentifully, as at Matata inland waters; where fern root of good quality was easily obtained, or where the sea teemed with fish, as at Tauranga.

Thus it happened that certain tribes became recognised as the producers of special kinds of food, and tribal nomenclature was not infrequently influenced thereby. In this way we find the Purukupenga (full net) living at Tauranga, the Waiohua (waters of abundance) at Rangitaiki and Matata, and other similar names will appear when I enumerate them.

Here let me mention *en passant* that about two hundred years after the Hawaikians had landed at Maketu, a portion of them,

viz., Tapuika and Waitaha a Hei, was attacked by the Waiohua, the Tipapa, and other hapus of Te Tini o Tannu or Ngaiwi tribe, the war being about land. I will not anticipate the particulars of the story, and will merely say now that the struggle was severe and ended in the defeat of the aborigines, who fled through Waikato to Tamaki and Waitakere, and that is how Ngaiwi, of whom the Waiohua were a part, came to live in the district now called Auckland. In those days the name Waitakere seems to have been used at a distance to denote the district north of the Tamaki, and was used in a general manner like Taranaki, Hauraki, Tauranga, etc. The subsequent history of the Waiohua is well known.

In war the aboriginal Maori was courageous. He is described as tall, spare, active, and with a good reach in the delivery of his weapon;[*] this, at any rate, is what is said of one of his war-like tribes, Te Rangihouhiri, now known as Ngaeterangi, who, at the battle of Poporohuamea, defeated the combined Hawaikian forces of Te Arawa, Takitumu, and Tainui, and taking Maketu from the former, advanced to Tauranga, which place they wrested from Ngatiranginui, who were also Hawaikian by Takitumu origin. The aboriginal Maori built pas in strong positions, having ramparts that were often extensive. Sometimes earthworks were thrown up to divide the pa into two or more sections, which would seem to show that while the hapus combined against the common enemy they had to guard against each other.

There is nothing to show that the aboriginal practised cannibalism or that he offered human sacrifices in war, whereas the Hawaikian Maori when he came to these shores did both.

The aboriginal Maori believed in the tra-

[*] The ancient inhabitants hunted the moa until it became extinct. The last bird was killed with a taiaha by a man at Tarawera. The habits of the moa are described as solitary, living in pairs in secluded valleys in the depths of the forest near a running stream. It fed on shoots, roots, and berries, and was particularly fond of nikau and tree fern. It was supposed to feed at night, for it was never seen to eat in the daytime. Hence the proverb 'moa kai hau' as it always seemed to have its head in the air, catching wind. The moa had a plume of feathers on the top of its head. In the depths of the Motu forest there is a mountain called Moanui where, no doubt, the bird was killed by the people of Rotonui-a-wai and Wharikiri, for their descendants knew fifty years ago that their forefathers had slain the moa.

‡ The kakapo betrayed itself at night time by its cry. With the assistance of a dog it was easily caught. Only within the present century did it become extinct, through constant hunting. Its loss, as a source of food, was very much felt by the Maoris.

‡ Kao was a favourite article of diet made by drying the karaka berry and the kumera root.

§ The rat was, perhaps, the most valued kind of Maori game; when in season the flesh was greatly relished. They were kept in rat runs or preserves, which no stranger would venture to poach upon.

[*] In draining a swamp some time ago at Knighton, the estate of S. Seddon, Esq., near Hamilton, Waikato, two wooden swords, believed to be of maire, were dug up in a good state of preservation, one 2ft the other 5ft below the surface. It would be interesting if we could be sure that these are ancient Maui Maori weapons, although I suppose there can be little doubt about it, for they differ entirely from any weapon used by the New Zealanders when Europeans first came amongst them. A man armed with a taiaha or tewhatewha would have but little difficulty in coping with the bearer of one of these swords—notwithstanding they are good weapons of their kind. One is a heavy cutting sword, the pitch of the handle bespeaks a circular movement. It has no guard, the length of the handle and size of grasp is the same as an English infantry officer's sword is, or used to be; the length of the blade is 10in shorter. This shows that the hand it was made for was as large as the hand of a man of the present time. The other sword, also without a guard, is two-edged and is apparently a thrust-sword. The idea of the stone mere seems to be developed from this ancient form of weapon. The swords are in the possession of Mr Seddon, junr., of Gorton, Cambridge.

dition of a Divine Incarnation, and he, of course, had faith in the supernatural power of such a Being. The narrative of how the child Oho manifested his Divine origin, when they met to do for him after their law (some authorities call the rite baptism),* is simple and beautiful, and is pitched upon a high plane of thought, compared with which the mythological ideas of the Hawaikians, who stole their atuas from one another and carried them about with them, are grovelling.

A feature in the life of this people was their partiality for bird pets. A bird that could talk well was prized by its owners and coveted by the neighbours, and this to such an extent that chiefs sometimes quarrelled, and on two occasions on the East Coast resort was had to war. I shall, at the proper time, tell of one of these wars and its unexpected outcome, for unless I do I am afraid that the origin of a tribe of aboriginal extraction now flourishing will be lost ; the survivors, if any, who know these things being few and reticent.

This ancient people has preserved its genealogies with care, tracing its ancestors back more than 1,000 years. Their tree contains double the number of generations found upon the tree of a Hawaikian subsequent to the immigration. It is an interesting field of enquiry to learn what (beyond the art of cultivation) the immigrants taught the aborigines, and what the latter acquired from the former in various forms of knowledge. There is no doubt that the manners, customs, religion, polity and the arts of the two peoples have been fused by time and habit into the civilisation belonging to one nation now ; the process, however, has left its marks, some of which are easily seen. Thus the aboriginal tribes that remain intact have almost invariably adopted the Hawaikian prefix to their names. The Hawaikian gave up the use of tappa clothing, and ceased to plant the aute tree round his pa because the flax garments of the country suited him better, they could be made at all times, whereas the tappa cloth was too frequently unobtainable for years after the invasion of a hostile army, as it was a maxim in war, if a pa could not be taken, to destroy the cultivations, and cut down the aute trees. The aborigines knew nothing about ocean-

* When the child Oho was being tuatia-ed, and prayer that he might be brave and strong in war, and strong in peace to cultivate the ground and perform the many functions of social life was being made, he stretched forth his hand and took the sacred food offered to the Deity and ate it. His two brothers perceiving the fearful thing called their father, who, when he saw the demeanour and action of the child became aware that he was of Divine origin, and said to his sons, 'The child is not one of us, it is his own food that he is eating.'

going canoes and how to build them, until they were taught by men from Hawaiki. Three natives of that country were cast upon the coast one night, their companions having been lost with their canoe. The people of Toi, at Whakatane, succoured them, and they in turn showed how to build 'Te Aratawhao' canoe which sailed to Hawaiki to fetch kumara and taro. This was before the immigrants came from Hawaiki.

The tribal nomenclature of the aborigines, as far as is known, was for the most part borrowed from the names of natural objects, not excluding favourite kinds of food. It differed from that used by the people from Hawaiki in not recognising by a prefix the descent of a tribe from an ancestor. They had before their tribal name no Ngati, Ngae, Aetanga, Uri, or Whanau, and where the Nga appeared it would seem to have been susceptible of another meaning. Some of these names were very beautiful and quite unique, as the 'Small Leaved Tawa Tree,' the 'Waving Fronds of the Tree Fern' ; others were descriptive as the 'Tribe of the Rocks,' the 'Go As You Please or 'Travel Easily' ; and other names were such as the 'Red Crab' the 'Creature Crouchant,' the 'Curling Wave,' the 'Thickly Standing Fern,' and so on.

It will be twenty years next August since I first drew the attention of the public to the existence of this interesting race. Speaking at a meeting of the Philosophical Society at Wellington, I said that the people who came to this country in the canoes found the land inhabited, that the men of the island were hospitable to the Hawaikians, and the latter intermarried with the former ; but when, in course of some two hundred years, the immigrants had become strong, wars ensued in many parts, and the aborigines were often destroyed ; that these wars, however, were not universal, and where the natives had lived at peace the races had amalgamated. A report of the proceedings was published in the local papers at the time.

I will now give the names of the tribes and hapus of the Maui Maori nation that have been furnished to me by the natives themselves, also the districts where they are, or where they lived formerly, also a short account of each hapu or tribe in so far as I am able, and the same may have sufficient interest.

Te Tini o Taunu, also known as Ngaiwi, known too as Te Tini o Awa (Awa was the human brother of Oho before mentioned)—but not to be confounded with Te Tinio Awa, a chief of Ngatipukenga—lived in the Bay of Plenty, between Rangitaiki and Tauranga. There were many hapus in this tribe ; namely, Waiohua, Tipapa, Haeremariri, Raupungaoheohe, Papakawhero

Tururu Mauku, Tawarauririki, Rarauhi Turuhunga, Ngaru Tauwharewharenga, and Purukupenga. This tribe, or group of tribes, fought against the Arawa, or some of them, but the two last named hapus are not mentioned as having taken part in the strife, nor do I know what became of them eventually.

It was twelve generations ago (say, 360 years) that that war took place. The Waiohua and Tipapa were incensed at the encroachments of Tapuika, then the rangatira hapu of the Arawa, whose chief was Marukukere; battles ensued, in which the Tapuika were defeated although assisted by Waitaha a Hei, another hapu of the Arawa, who lived on the eastern shores of Tauranga. Many chiefs, including Marukukere, were slain, and the Arawa were in such straits that they sought aid from their compatriots at Taupo. Moko-tangatatahi led the army that came to their assistance from Wharepuhunga at Titi-raupenga. He was an energetic young chief, and nephew to Marukukere. The struggle, however, was protracted and the issue doubtful when Moko consulted Kaiongonga, a noted priest, who, to attain his ends, demanded a human sacrifice, who must be a man of rank. The demand was complied with, and Tangarengare, a senior relative of Moko, was given up for the public good. The courage of the victim acted as an incentive to the people, and stimulated them so that they vanquished their enemies at Punakauia; then Te Tini fled and became scattered, and were destroyed in detail, but some remnants of Te Waiohua and other hapus of Ngaiwi escaped to Waikato, where they had friends, and from there they went to Tamaki and Waitakere, and occupied the district now called Auckland. This happened about 150 years before the chief Hua, of Te Waiohua, flourished at One Tree Hill pa, near One-hunga, and the supposition is erroneous that the Waiohua are named after him. The natives who furnished the evidence to the Native Land Court upon which that opinion was based were either ignorant of the history and origin of Te Waiohua, which is not improbable considering it is usually the victor, not the vanquished, who cherishes the tradition of war and destruction, to the one it is a glory, to the other a shame; or they suppressed the information as unnecessary to their case. This practice is not at all uncommon, and sometimes all the parties to a suit will agree to avoid fees and shorten labour by eliminating a few chapters of history considered by them to have little or no bearing on the points at issue.

It is said that some of Ngaiwi travelled as far as the Bay of Islands, which is quite likely, as the tribe of Ngatirahiri lived in the North then, who were of Awa origin, and would naturally be disposed to be friendly towards them. Here let me explain who the Ngatirahiri were. Shortly after the arrival of Mataatua at Whaka-tane, Rahiri, a leading man amongst the immigrants, made a plantation on the hill side overhanging the mouth of the river. When he had planted there awhile his two younger brothers quarrelled with him, and forcibly ejecting him from the cultivation, took possession of it themselves. Rahiri, unable to brook the insult, determined to leave his relatives and make a home elsewhere. He had formed a friendly connection with some aborigines of the Toi tribe (of Awa descent though not of Te Tini o Awa), by whom he was advised to go to Hokianga or the Bay of Islands. Accompanied by certain of these aborigines he went and founded a tribe in the North that bears his name to this day, and is really a cross of Awa blood aboriginal and imported. It is supposed that aboriginal Awa were living in the North prior to the movement of Rahiri and his party, and that it was the knowledge of this that influenced them in the choice of their new home.

The Tapuika-Ngaiwi war conferred an unwelcome legacy upon the victors in the form of an undying feud between Tapuika and Ngatimoko about the divison of the land they had conquered. The former thought the latter grasped the fruits of victory too much, the latter considered the former unreasonable, and refused to give way. The ill feeling has been handed down through three centuries of time to the present generation. We shall see by-and-by that another Hawaikian tribe managed to avoid this difficulty by the expedient of dividing the lands of the aborigines amongst themselves before conquest.

Ngatiawa is the tribal name of the immigrants who came to New Zealand in Mataatna canoe. The name Awa is, however, aboriginal as well as Hawaikian, and was acquired in time past by the former through Awanui a Rangi, a younger branch of Toi family. The Ngatiawa (immigrant race) had no wars with the aboriginal Awa (Toi) east of Whakatane as far as inland Motu; but to the southward and westward it was different. On those sides they displaced the aboriginal element, when they had become strong enough to do so. This is how the Ngaiwi in course of time were thrust up against Tapuika and compelled to fight that tribe; how the whole of the Uriwera district was over-run and occupied by Ngaetuhoe, a tribe of Ngatiawa.

Another tribe who appear to have been aboriginal was Ngamarama. They lived originally at Matamata* and other places in the Upper Thames Valley, whence they moved to Tauranga, and occupied the central and western portions of that district. They were a numerous people at the time the canoes came from Hawaiki too numerous, and uninviting probably, for the immigrants by Takitumu to remain when they visited Te Awanui, the name Tauranga harbour was known by then, on their way to the South. One or two of the crew, however, did leave the canoe and settle amongst the Ngamarama, thus a link was formed between the descendants of those immigrants in the south and Ngamarama that resulted in the conquest of Ngamarama and the taking of Tauranga by Ngatiranginui several generations afterwards. There is a remnant of Ngamarama still living at Te Irihanga at Tauranga; it is known by the name of Ngatirangi, and is not to be confused with Ngaeterangi, who destroyed Ngatiranginui, and are dominant now at Tauranga.

In respect to Tua Rotorua tribe, who lived at Rotorua, tradition is conflicting, but the balance of evidence is, I think, in favour of their aboriginal extraction; it is not so much a question of whether the chief of that people had Arawa (immigrant) blood in his veins, a thing by no means improbable, considering his reputed grandparent had travelled that way to Wanganui, as it is a question whether the Arawa or any of them would have waged without cause a war of extermination against a branch of their own tribe; judging from their history we may say unhesitatingly that even with a *casus belli* such a thing would not have been thought of, and an utu account properly balanced would have been considered sufficient to serve all purposes of revenge, especially if supplemented with the acquisition of a little land. But in the war of the Arawa against Tua Rotorua if they did not succeed in annihilating the latter it was not for want of trying. The remnant of this aboriginal tribe is the Ngatitura now living where the Oxford Road emerges from the forest on the side towards Rotorua; the trackless, waterless forest has been their friend, and to it they

owe their existence. Here let me instance the different degrees of animus that characterised ancient Maori warfare as between immigrant tribes and aboriginal, and as between the immigrants themselves. Take the aboriginal group of tribes known as Te Tini o Taunu or Ngaiwi, of whom the Waiohua were a part. Such of these tribes as escaped annihilation were driven completely out of their native district—first by Mataatua and then by Arawa immigrants. The refugees of Tuarotorua only saved themselves by sheltering in Patetere Forest, as did Ngamarama when driven out of Tauranga by Ngatiranginui, an immigrant tribe from Hangaroa River, south of Tuaranga, whose forefathers had come to New Zealand in Takitumu canoe. And yet again we find tribes of these races fighting to the death when Te Rangihouhiri drove out Tapuika and took and settled Maketu, nor were the efforts of all Hawaikians far and near sufficient to dislodge them. Tematera from Hauraki, Whakane from Rotorua, and Waitaha a Hei and Ranginui from Tauranga, were all driven off and defeated when they attempted to aid the Tapuika. Here we have an instance of tribes of Hawaikians, of Arawa, Tainui and Takitumu origin combining against the aboriginal people, and combining unsuccessfully. Then in a little while, that is to say within the same generation, Te Rangihouhiri advanced from Maketu to Tauranga, and well nigh exterminated Waitaha a Hei and Ngatiranginui. The survivors of the former escaped to the Arawa at the lakes, and a small remnant of the latter found a refuge in the same forest that they had driven the poo remains of the Ngamarama to; thus history repeated herself with a vengeance, and the two remnants live almost side by side at the present time. The name of the Ngamarama remnant has already been given as Ngatirangi. The name of Ngatiranginui remnant is Te Pirirakau (Stick in the Bush), which shows pretty plainly how closely they hid themselves from the conquering Ngaeterangi, who had taken possession of Tauranga.

Now the intertribal struggles of the Hawaikians cannot be compared with these wars 'a mort.' Take the lake district. The wars between the east and west ends of Rotoiti, between the north and south ends of Rotorua, the feud between Moko and Tapuika, the differences between the legitimate and bastard branches of the people on the east side, and anything that may have occurred on the west, have none of them resulted in anything more than a little killing and eating from time to time, and then mending matters by a peacemaking. Only at the south end of Rotorua, in a struggle between the people occupying

*The present European Matamata and Railway Station of that name are several miles away from the true Matamata, which is at the European settlement now called Waharoa. The Matamata pa, a large one, stood beside the river, and was some little distance westward and northward from the C.M.S. Mission Station, which my father helped to found in 1835. The Mission Station was a little to the southward of where the Waharoa Railway Station now stands. The line seems to run through the site of the old station. Waharoa is a new name for that land, borrowed probably from the chief of that name, whose story I published in 1866, and given by Europeans who appropriated the historical name of Matamata for their own settlement many miles off.

two lakes, do we find that some land has changed hands, of which the area is small compared with the rest of the landed estate of the losers, nor in this war was there any apparent intention on either side to proceed to extremities.

Leaving the Arawa, whose name in ancient times, I ought to say, was Nga oho Matakamokamo, and whose motto was, ' Oho tapu nui te Arawa,' let us turn to the Ngatiawa, of Mataatua canoe. There is a civil war in the ancient history of this people. Te Kareke, a flourishing tribe descended from Uemua, of Mataatua, were driven away from Te Poroa, in the Upper Whakatane Valley, by Ngaetonu, now called Ngatipukeko. They fled eastward, where many became absorbed amongst the aboriginal Whakatohea. Estimated by its results, this may be considered an exceptionally severe case of civil war amongst the Hawaikians. The same Ngaetonu drove the aboriginal Irawharo away to the westward ; this war lasted a long time, and there were many campaigns in it. Eventually the Irawharo found shelter with their compatriots, the Rangihouhiri, at Tauranga, where their little remnant still exists. Here I would note that while including the Irawharo amongst the aborigines, I do not mean to say they were not also of Hawaikian origin. It would be quite impossible now to draw a hard and fast line, and say, here is where the blood of the old race ends, and there is where the new blood begins, especially eastward of Whakatane, where the two are very intermixed, and it should be known that Ngatirawharo came from Ohiwa, which was their birth-place as a tribe ; but the difficulty attending a line of demarcation does not interfere with the general grouping of the tribes according to race, and according to position, surroundings, and sides taken where relationships were mingled.

I might continue to compare the bitter character of the war of race on the one hand with the milder form of domestic strife on the other, and explain exceptional cases by the circumstances preceding them ; but it is hardly worth while to do so, seeing that each war will be presented at the proper time, when the reader can judge for himself whether the remarks offered and examples given should have a wider application ; for myself, I think it can be shown by analysis of the cause and circumstances of each war, that the rule applies to the greater portion, if not to the whole, of Te Ika a Maui Island.

I will now return from this disquisition to the description of the Maui Maori tribes. There was a great tribe known by the name of Toi who, before the canoes came from Hawaiki, and at that time occupied a large part of Te Ika a Maui, extending from Whakatane eastwards. I might mention Toi in a general way as an ancestor over a very wide country ; but it is not in that sense that I use the name now. I refer instead to the tribe of Toi proper, whose country extended from Whakatane to inland Motu. I would, however, observe first that though we have a Hawaikian Awa and an aboriginal Awa, also Hawaikian and aboriginal Oho tribes, we have no Hawaikian Toi tribe in New Zealand, only the aboriginal Toi is to be found in Te Ika a Maui ; and yet in the genealogies of each nation the names of these three ancestors are found standing in the closest relationship at a time long before the passage of the canoes. The Maui Toi lived nearly 200 years, and the Hawaiki Toi 400 years before the migration. I cannot tell how it is that these important names are common to the two nations. It might be asked how was their language the same ? and how did it happen that they were of a similar appearance ? If we could answer these questions we should have the key to much besides.

A principal pa of Toi was Kapu, situated on the highest point of the Whakatane hills, as seen from the mouth of the river. Hokianga, at Ohiwa, was a fishing station. Tawhitirahi, overlooking Kukumoa stream, was a very strong pa ; another of their places was Kohipaua, east of the Otara River, and they had a settlement at Te Rotonuiawai at inland Motu, and doubtless they had kaingas and pas at intermediate places. As already stated, this people were of the aboriginal Awa stock.

The head man at Motu at a certain time was Tauwharanui. He lived at Te Rotonui awai, near Whakapaupakihi River. It happened that a strange man came to his kainga one day, who said that his name was Tarawa, and that he was a god. When asked how he claimed to be a god, he said that he had swam across the ocean to this country, and that no one unpossessed of supernatural power could do that thing. Then he remained at the kainga and married Manawakaitu, the daughter of Tauwharangi, by whom he had two children. But Tauwharangi failed to discern any Divine attributes in his son-in-law, and sceptically awaited an opportunity to prove his power by ocular demonstration. At length a chance occurred, and one night Tarawa was awakened from sleep by water coming into his bed. He arose to find a flood had suddenly covered the land, and that all had fled. His retreat was cut off, and he had to climb to the top of his house and call for help to the others who, knowing the local signs, had avoided the danger, and by their chief's order had left him unwarned. He was told to save himself. He said he could not perform an impossibility. 'O! but you can easily save yourself by your Divine power.' It then came out that he was not a god at all, and that they must send a canoe and save him, which they did. Old Tauwharangi was so disgusted that he thrust Tarawa out of the kainga, and told his daughter that if she went with him she must leave the children. She departed with her husband, and they settled a few miles away at Te Wharekiri, on Motohora Mountain, overlooking the valley of the Motu. Here they lived and died, and here they left a family that has now expanded into the important hapu of Ngaitama, of the Whakatohea tribe. This hapu is therefore of mixed aboriginal and immigrant blood, for there is no doubt but that Tarawa left one of the canoes during its passage along the coast, as Taritoringo left Tainui at Hawai and found his way to inland Motu, and like the woman Torere, who swam ashore from Tainui at night as the canoe was passing Taumata-Apanui point; also like some of the passengers by Takitumu, who left her en route, and whose blood now flows in the veins of some of the principal chiefs inland of Ohiwa, and from whom the Ngatira hapu of the Whakatohea are partially descended.

From Tauwharanui's two grandchildren, whom their parents had left with him when they went to Motohora, and from others no doubt of his hapu or family, sprang the Ngatingahere, another hapu of the Whakatohea, and in after times Ngatipatu, another hapu branched from the Ngatingahere.

Again, when Mataatua arrived at Whakatane with Ngatiawa immigrants from Hawaiki, Muriwai, the old woman who headed the party, had a son named Repanga. From the top of Whakatane range this man descried the smoke of the aborigines at Kohipawa. He returned to his mother, told her what he had seen, and obtained permission to visit the people. Arrived at Kohipawa, he was hospitably received by Ranginui te Kohu, the chief of that place, whose daughter, Ngapupereta, he married. From; this source at Kohipawa sprang Ngatirua, another hapu of the Whakatohea, being the fifth and last hapu of the great tribe of the Whakatohea, all of which are of mixed extraction, three being tinged with Tainui strain, one with Ngatiawa, and one with a Takitumu connection.

We have seen that Torere left Tainui at Taumata Apanui—this she did to avoid the addresses of Rakataura, one of the crew. Arrived on shore, she concealed herself in the bush in a valley, the stream in which bears her name still. The next morning when her flight was discovered, Rakataura

landed, and returning along the shore passed Torere and Taumata Apanui, searching in vain for the woman. Then he gave it up, and turned and followed his companions by land, whom he at length rejoined at Kawhia. Torere joined affinity with the aborigines in that locality, and Ngaitai, a tribe that takes its name from her canoe, represents the union then formed; and this tribe is acknowledged by Tainui authority to be one that belongs to their own connection.

An interesting illustration of practical tradition is furnished in connection with this Ngaitai tribe. Although the tribe has a very ancient genealogical record extending some twelve generations back beyond the immigration from Hawaiki, and believed itself to be thoroughly rangatira, yet it was unable satisfactorily to define its origin. The question was raised to their humiliation during a boundary dispute by the Whakatohea in 1844, when Rangimatauuku, chief of Ngatirua, speaking of the land in question and its ownership, said to Eru, the chief of Ngaitai, at a great meeting at Opape (that was convened by my father in the hope to settle the dispute without bloodshed), 'Who are you? I know the chiefs of Ngatiawa, and Te Uriwera, the canoe they came in, and how they obtained their possessions. I know Te Whanau Apanui, who they are, and how they occupy. Also, I know whom we, the Whakatohea, are; but I do not know who you are. Tell me the name of your canoe?'

Challenged thus, Eru was compelled to say something in self-defence, and replied, 'We came in your canoe.'

'Oh!' said Rangimatanuku, 'you came in my canoe, did you? I did not see you there, I know all who came in my canoe; all who came in the bow and all in the stern. If you were on board you must have been somewhere out of sight, down in the bilge I suppose, bailing out the water.

Rangimatanuku was a chief of note, and was no doubt very well informed in Maori lore, and if so, his speech betrays the pride the Maori of his time had in Hawaikean descent, which is suggestive of a superiority of the immigrant, not only in his possession of seed and the art of cultivation, but as having personal qualities such as tact and address, skill at sea, and a knowledge of war on shore. As a a rule, Hawaikian blood has been more thought of, and this has led many natives and many tribes unconsciously astray in figuring to themselves their ancient history. A fact cannot be ignored for generations with impunity, sooner or later it will become diminished in men's minds, or lost sight of altogether. Not that I have ever found a native ashamed of an aboriginal connection; far from it, but his other side seems always to be more present to him, more engrained, so to speak, in his being and memory.

Only once have I heard a Mani Maori speak in public with great and real pride of his unique and ancient descent. That was when the chief of Uepohatu or Iwi Pohatu a Maui put the land of his tribe at Hiku-rangi Mountain, Waiapu, through the Native Land Court of New Zealand, and obtained a legal title to it. On that occa-sion the chief (Wi Tahata) said that he was descended from Maui, from whom he claimed. He gave his genealogy 38 genera-tions from Maui. He spoke of the Hawai-kians as having come to their island in canoes from across the sea in an age long after the time that they, the Maori nation, had peopled it. He showed the boundaries of the territory that belonged to his section of the Maori nation before the Hawakians came, and the inroads that had since been made upon them, and he asked me as the Judge of that Court, to accompany him to the top of the mountain, there to view his his ancestors' canoe in its rocky form, a proceeding, however, which to the Court seemed unnecessary.

It was reserved for me to tell the Ngaitai the name of the canoe they are connected with, and I got my information from first-class Tainui authority in the Tainui country.

Beyond Taumata Apanui, at Hawai, lived the aboriginal tribe Te Manu Koau, who were conquered and scattered by Te Whanau Apanui, which is a tribe of mixed origin, being partly of Ngatiawa and partly Pororangi blood (i.e., of Mataatua and Takitunu), but all of Hawaikian ex-traction. This tribe now lives on the land thus taken. As for the remnant of Te Manu Koau it fled through the mountains, and came to Raukumara Mountain in Hicks' Bay district. Here the refugees were discovered by the tribe of Tuwhakai-riora, who killed and ate a number of them, but when Tu te Rangiwhiu became aware of what was taking place he interposed, and rescued them and made slaves of them, setting them to work to catch the birds of that mountain. Tu te Rangiwhiu was the chief of the Tuwhakairiora tribe at that time, now some three hundred years ago. Those slaves have been working there ever since. I have seen them myself, and was much impressed with their timid, deprecating cringing air, and exceedingly rough exterior. The man who placed them in bondage was a Hawaikian.

And now I come to the Iwi Pohatu a Maui, or Uepohatu, as they now call them-selves, to whom I have just referred. They live at Tuparoa, also they reside at the foot of Hikurangi, their antipodean Ararat, whose summit is shrouded in snow in

winter, and they have land at Raukumara. Formerly their landed possessions were continuous between these points, and their sea frontage extended from Tuparoa to Waiapu River. This was a domain per-haps 40 miles long and 15 wide. However, Ngatiporou (who are Hawaikians of Taki-tunu), one way or other, have now got the greater part of it: but the tribe has al-ways been free, is now intact, and holds the residue of its lands in independence, and is, moreover, recognised by the sur-rounding tribes of Hawaikian extraction as being aboriginal and of Maui descent.

Adjoining Uepohatu country to the west was a group of five aboriginal tribes. Their habitat extended from Waiapu to Potikirua, near Cape Runaway.

These were the Ngaoko at Horoera Hekawa, and Kawakawa.

The Ruawaipu at Pukeamaru and Whare-kahika (Hicks' Bay).

And the three hapus of Parariki, viz., Parariki proper, Ngaituiti, and Ngaitu-moana. The prefixes to the two latter names are probably of Hawaikian origin. These three hapus occupied the country between Wharekahika and Potikirua, Ngaituiti being at the Wharekahika end of the district, and Ngaitumoana at the Poti-kirua, or western end.

Rather more than four hundred years ago, Ngaoko for some reason attacked Ruawaipu and destroyed them. But a young chieftainess named Tamateaupoko escaped to Whangara, where he married Ue-kaihau, of Pororangi tribe, a chief amongst the immigrants, and a descendant of Pai-kea, the captain who brought Takitunu from Hawaiki to Whangara, near Gisborne, about six hundred years ago.

In due time three sons, Uetaha, Tama-koro, and Tahania, the issue of this mar-riage, grew up, and determined to avenge the death of their grandfather and the overthrow of his tribe. They organised a strong force of the people of Takitunu canoe, thereafter known as Ngaituere, and set out by land along the coast. At Ten-gatoetoe the Aetangahanti endeavoured to stop their way, but were defeated in pitch battle; again, at Tawhiti, Te Wahineiti attempted to bar their pro-gress. and were also defeated. For the rest of their march they were unopposed until they encountered the offending Nga-oko, whom they vanquished in a series of engagements and seiges rather ~~rather~~ more than three hundred and fifty years ago. Ngaoko were scattered and killed, their remnant reduced to captivity, and their lands were appropriated by Ngaituere, who remained in undisputed possession until Tuwhakairiora and his followers appeared upon the scene some sixty years after-wards. At this time, therefore (about 1530

A.D.), the Hawaikian people held the country from the mouth of the Waiapu River to Wharekahika, and the aborigines continued to hold from the latter place to Potikirua.

When Tuwhakairiora, who was a young chief descended from Pororangi, of Hawaikian extraction, appeared, things became changed; not only did he subjugate Ngaituere who had attacked him wantonly, but the three hapus of Parariki that had maintained their independence hitherto were disturbed by him. Parariki proper and Ngaetumoana were driven from their holdings westward to Whangaparaoa, and the third, Ngaituiti, from which he had married a wife, Ruatanpare, was reduced to a condition dependent upon himself. Of this extraordinary chief, his origin and education, his mission, his wars and conquests, his revenge, and of the tribe bearing his name that now occupies the country between Te Kautuku and Potikirua—that is to say, from between Waiapu and the East Cape to between Point Lottin and Cape Runaway, I may speak more particularly later on in this narrative.

I have said that Tuwhakairiora married Ruataupare; the manner in which he married this, his first wife, bespoke the dominant character of the man. Travelling alone, he arrived for the first time on the shore of Wharekahika Bay, and there he saw two young women in the water collecting shell fish. Their clothes were on the beach. He sat upon them. After waiting long in the water for the stranger to continue his journey, the women, who were cold and ashamed, came in from the sea and asked for their garments. He gave them up, and told the young women to take him to their parents' kainga. The women were Ruataupare and Anahi Koata, her sister. On the way to the kainga he told Anahi that he intended to take Ruataupare to wife, an event that speedily came to pass. He was aware of the identity of the women when he sat on their clothes.

That marriage did not turn out well. Ruataupare considered herself ill used, and left her husband. She went to her relatives at Tokomaru (she was half Kahukuranui), where she lived and died. She conquered that district from the Wahineiti. The tribe living at Tokomaru bears her name to this day.

We read in the journal of his voyage that it was here, at Tokomaru, that Cook first held friendly intercourse with the New Zealanders. The place was, to say the least, of an antochthonous atmosphere, and we may not unreasonably assume it was here that that great navigator received an answer to a question that must have been uppermost in his mind when he was told that the name of the country he had come to was Ehinomaui.

Had he asked the same question at a purely immigrant settlement such as Maketu, Mercury Bay, or the Thames, he would doubtless have been informed that the name was Aotearoa — Long White World. And why? simply because it was the name they had given to it when they arrived off the coast about 1290, A.D.—estimating a generation at 30 years—and having sailed along the strange shore for hundreds of miles were impressed with its extent and its white appearance. From the eastern precipices of the Great Barrier and Mercury Islands to the beaches and headlands of the Bay of Plenty, and from Te Mahia to past the East Cape, all the coast line was more or less white in colour as the eastern summer sun shone upon it. The few dark rocks only brought the white into relief, and increased the impression, and they were partially hidden too by the foliage of the pohutukawa tree, that was not to know the white man's axe for several hundred years to come. Thus history in her unceasing round repeated her recurrent ways, and the ancient Britain of the South became another Albion to another band of strangers who came to occupy her soil.

The Whatumamoa were another tribe of aboriginal Maoris. They lived at Hawke's Bay, near Napier; one of their principal pas was Te Heipipi, near Petane, and they had a pa near Taradale, and other pas. This tribe was attacked by a section of the descendants of the immigrants by Takitumu canoe, who came under Teraia from Nukutaurua. They fought against Te Heipipi pa, but were unable to take it on account, as they believed, of the antochthon god of the pa being superior to their own god; therefore they made peace with Te Heipipi, but they took some other Whatumamoa pas, and eventually the residue of the aborigines became absorbed in the Takitumu people, now known as Ngatikahungungu.

A tribe of aborigines called Te Tauira lived at Wairoa, Hawke's Bay, who were numerous and had many pas. Their principal pa was at Rakautihia. They were attacked by a section of the Takitumu people, who having got into trouble at home, had migrated from Turanga to Waihau, on the Hangaroa. This party was led by Rakaipaka and Hinemanuhiri. They lived awhile at Waihau, and there under some provocation made war on Te Tauira, and to prevent quarrels after conquest they apportioned the lands of Te Tauira amongst themselves before the war commenced. The war resulted in the complete conquest and expatriation of the Tauira tribe, whose refugees fled to

Hawke's Bay and Wairarapa, where some hapus of their tribe lived. The only person saved by Rakaipaka was a woman named Hinekura. He saved her because he had had an intrigue with her before the trouble began. In this war it was, at the battle of Taupara, that the Tauira tribe was crushed.

Lastly, a large tribe of Maui Maoris, named Te Marangaranga, inhabited Te Whaiti country. They were destroyed by the descendants of the immigrants of Mataatua canoe.

I have now covered the ground from the Upper Thames to Hawke's Bay, inclusive, by the East Coast, and far back into the interior to the middle of the island nearly; excepting two gaps on the coast, namely, from north of Te Mahia to south of Tuparoa (Te Tanira occupied Te Mahia), and from Potikirua, near Cape Runaway, to Maraenui. I have not the information in respect to the ancient inhabitants of these two areas necessary to enable me to state with precision who they were and what became of them. We all know, however, that (excepting lands alienated to Europeans) the former is held entirely by the descendants of Hawaikians, that is, of the men who landed at Whangara from Takitumu with Paikea, their captain, who very likely fixed on that locality because he saw no aborigines there. Into the latter, as we have seen, Ngaetumoana and Parariki proper were driven by Tuwhakairiora. We also know that Ngatiawa are living in that district now under the names of Ngaetawarere and Whanau Ihutu. There is, therefore, perhaps, to some extent, an admixture of the aboriginal element in those tribes. I am not, however, able to affirm anything, having never travelled in their country, nor had opportunity to inquire—and in covering the ground named I have covered the whole of three spheres of influence—namely, of the three canoes, Takitumu, Mataatua, and Arawa, in so far as the relations of the immigrants with the aborigines are concerned. This qualification is necessary, because I am not now treating of wars that took place in remote parts of the island between the outpost colonies of the various canoes, such as the war between Tainui and Arawa people at

Taupo four hundred years ago, when the latter ousted the former from the south and east sides of the lake, or the wars between the people of Takitumu and Tainui after that at Moawhango and the Upper Rangitikei Rivers, when the latter were again expelled. These wars amongst the descendants of the immigrants in remote parts were bitter struggles for territory; not mere tribal strife with an utu account, and they usually ended in one side being crushed and driven off.

The same thing took place between Ngatiawa of Mataatua, and Ngatiporou of Takitumu; their theatre of war was about Te Kaha, where there were many campaigns. Te Kaha pa obtained its name from the number of sieges it withstood in that war.

In determining dates, I have estimated a generation at 30 years' duration, which period, all circumstances considered, seems pretty reasonable as a chronological standard. Of course, any estimate of this sort is necessarily arbitrary. The reader, however, can reduce it if he thinks the unit too large; at the same time, it is well to remember that many Maori chiefs had many succeeding wives, and the genealogies preserved embrace not infrequently the youngest born of the youngest as well as the first born of the first wife, nor had the latter a monopoly of distinction. Twhakairiora, Tuhourangi, Tutanekai, Hinemoa, and others were all youngest or nearly youngest children, yet each is a prominent figure in Maori tradition.

In concluding this sketch in the history of the autochthons of New Zealand, let me say that all the facts set forth have been imparted to me by the Maoris themselves, excepting, as already stated, such things as I learned from my father in the forties. He prosecuted his inquiries in the thirties and forties, and was one of the very few in those early times who took an interest in the history, laws, and customs of the Maoris. Before his death he wrote to me from England urging me to publish my information on these subjects.

My next chapter will be upon the voyage of the Hawaikians from their own country to New Zealand.

THE HAWAIKI MAORI IMMIGRATION.

THE story of the immigration from Hawaiki, as told fifty years ago and more by old natives, was that their ancestors had left that country in consequence of disputes chiefly about land; that the land available for cultivation was not extensive, and increasing population had created a pressure that resulted in wars for the possession of it — these troubles lasted more or less a long time, during which their party was gradually weakened and overpowered; that terms had then been proposed to them, namely, that they must leave Hawaiki and seek another home across the sea, and that ample time to build a flotilla and make all necessary preparations for departure would be allowed to them. They accepted these terms in the spirit in which they were offered, and preparations were made in a careful and methodical manner.

I think the whole scope of action at Hawaiki at this juncture strongly indicates a knowledge of the existence and whereabouts of another country to which the emigrants might go. The very terms, their acceptance, and the confidence with which the equipment was made, all betoken such knowledge; nor is there anything in the whole story, so far as I am aware, to show that they were groping in the dark. Moreover, the result of the action justifies this remark. The direction, precision, and success of their navigation show, speaking colloquially, that the emigrants knew what they were about.

Now, if this were so, whence came this knowledge? This question is susceptible of several answers. For instance, the knowledge may have been handed down by tradition, that in a certain direction there was a distant country, the birthplace of their race, and from which they had travelled in bygone ages, when the sea was less continuous, and before intermediate lands had sunk under its waves. But if the latter part of this speculation is rejected, as perhaps it may—crust motions of the earth being slow and human memory short—still the former part remains feasible, because the common origin of the Hawaikian Maori and the Maui Maori peoples is manifest philologically, mythologically, and otherwise, and demands a point of union in the past. The name Rarotonga has a meaning, and tells how the ancient mariner who gave the island that name was impressed by the phenomenon observed during his voyage towards the north of the continually diminishing altitude in the southern heavens of the great stars that revolve round the Pole, and, as he advanced, of their disappearance below the horizon when on the meridian below the Pole; so that by the time he had discovered the island to which he gave that name, these stars were dipped below the sea a considerable time during that meridian passage, and he would be the more impressed by the unaccountable change because he was accustomed to estimate his latitude by the altitude at the passage named of the star Matatuotonga— The Watchful of the South. It is quite easy, therefore, to understand how the name may have been given, and whence the discoverer came. Conversely, had the voyager approached from the north, he would have named the island Rungatonga.

Again, if the Maui Maori people broke off from their countrymen at Hawaiki, why did they leave the art of cultivation behind them? These considerations favour the idea that a tradition of the nature outlined was extant at Hawaiki, and that it prompted successful exploration before emigration took place. Exploration could hardly have been made in the absence of a tradition to guide the navigator; the chances on the areas to be visited and the points to be steered are too numerous against it. Thus, New Zealand subtends from Rarotonga an arc so small that an error either way of three fourths of a point on the compass would send the voyager wide of the mark, and he would pass the islands without seeing them. On the other hand, it must be admitted that, as canoes have no hold in the water and no weight to meet the ocean swell, they could not work to windward to explore, nor could they run to leeward, for fear of not getting back; therefore, their movements would be confined to a comparatively limited area while in the trade wind region. In adverting to these questions, I would interject the remark that canoes sailing in low latitudes towards the south must stand across the south-east trades on the port tack, and ought not to start from a point that is to leeward of their destination; and further, I would say that in leaving Rarotonga for New Zealand all these conditions would be fulfilled.

Having now stated the reasons which render the theory of an exploration prior to the emigration likely, I will turn to tradition on the subject. One tradition says that a canoe named Matawhaorua, of which Kupe was the captain, sailed from Hawaiki and arrived at New Zealand. Along the coast of the North Island she passed for a considerable distance, and then returned safe home and made a report concerning the land she had seen. Matawhaorua did not return to New Zealand. As the particulars of this tradition have been furnished by other writers, it is unnecessary that I should repeat them, especially as it is my object to publish in these few pages original matter only.*

Another tradition, to which I have already referred, tells of how on a stormy night a canoe from Hawaiki was wrecked on the coast of New Zealand, four miles to the west of Whakatane River. The next morning, the daughter of the chief of the pa at Kapu found three strange men bereft of clothing shivering on the shore, who said that they had come from a distant country in a canoe that had been wrecked that night, and that all their companions were drowned. The woman returned to her father, whose name was Toi, and told him what she had seen. Her father ordered the men to be brought to Kapu. When they arrived, food was set before the three men, whose names were Taukata, Hoaki, and Maku. The food was fish, fern root, and the fronds of the tree-fern; there was no kumara. The three men noticed this, and Taukata produced from his waist-belt some kao (dried kumara), which he crumbled into dust and mixed with water, making a drink. This he presented to Toi, who, when he had drunk, demanded, 'Where such food, fit for the gods, could be obtained.' The strangers all replied, 'From Hawaiki, the country we have come from.' Toi said : 'Alas ! I am not able to send across the ocean to Hawaiki.'

The strangers replied : 'O ! yes, you can ; you can build a canoe.'

Toi said : 'No ; there are no trees in this country large enough to make a canoe fit to brave the waves of the ocean.'

The strangers : 'We saw a tree in the bed of the river at the ford this morning which is quite large enough. A canoe can be made of it that would reach Hawaiki, and we can go and show the way and bring back kumaras to you.'

Toi replied : 'It is well said. A canoe shall be built.'

Then the tree (a totara) was raised out of its bed at the mouth of the Orini River, and out of it the canoe Aratawhao (Way through the Wilderness) was made, and sailed for Hawaiki. Taukata, Maku, and a crew went in her.

Hoaki was kept by Toi as a hostage for the safety of his people who went in the canoe. Tradition is silent as to whether the Aratawhao arrived at her destination. She never returned to New Zealand. Toi

slew his hostage, after waiting two years in disappointment, and, leaving Kapu, where he and poor Hoaki had so often vainly scanned the horizon for the longed-for canoe, he retired to Hokianga at Ohiwa, where he was living with his people some time afterwards when Mataatua canoe arrived at Whakatane.

Let us now revert to the people whom we left preparing to emigrate from Hawaiki. We may reasonably suppose that the canoes they had were similar to those used by their descendants several centuries afterwards, for smaller vessels would not have answered their purpose. A canoe that would carry fifty fighting men on a short expedition would not carry more than twenty adults on a deep sea voyage with safety, allowing them provisions for a month at the rate of 2lb of food each and a quart of water per diem, and carrying half a ton of seed and other belongings. The bulky seed taken was that of kumara and taro ; seeds of the karaka tree and of the hue gourd were also taken. The gourd, as I have said, was already in New Zealand, though how it came there, being apparently not indigenous, I am unable to say. Also, they took with them their valued dogs of Ngatoroirangi breed*, from the skins of which their dog-skin mats were woven, and they took the Maori rat on board, the same being game of the finest kind.

It is true that the Arawa (if a female accompanied each male) carried thirty persons, twenty of whom were adults ; of the remaining ten, who were young persons, some may have been very young. She must, therefore, have been a large canoe. That she carried as much as they dared to put on board we know, from the fact that some members of the party were left behind to follow in another canoe named Te Whatu Ranganuku, which landed them at Wairarapa. An account of this will be given at the proper time. No doubt, the temptation to the emigrants, in some instances, to overload was very great.

That the Hawaikians came to New Zealand from the tropics is proved by the tropical character of the plants they brought with them—kumara and taro are both of that character. The latter is especially so, in the fact that it never could be properly acclimatised to the change. For six hundred years the taro Maori always had to be grown artificially. Sand or gravel was dug from a pit and carried to the field and placed in a layer over the soil ; this drew the sun's rays and warmed the plant, which was, moreover, defended

*The above statements about Matawhaorua are not borrowed from any European writer. They were made to me by a chief of Ngatiawa, now deceased.

*The Ngatoroirangi dog was extinct before Europeans settled in New Zealand. It is not to be confounded with the Kuri Maori, which finally disappeared before European breeds, about the middle forties.

from cutting winds by rows of manuka branches fixed in the ground at intervals. The same remarks in a much less degree apply to the kumara*.

I think I have shown now that the Hawaikians, when they embarked in their canoes, left some place in the tropics, and steered to the south-west across the south-east trade, and that they were probably provisioned for one month. The question, therefore, arises now, where did they sail from? To this the reply is, from Raro-tonga, which island is within the tropics and in a north-easterly direction from New Zealand, the distance between being about 1,500 geographical miles. Now, the Arawa and Tainui, as we shall presently learn, were each of them coasting along the shores of New Zealand about a fortnight, searching for sites for settlement, before their voyages ended at Maketu and Kawhia. This leaves, say, fifteen days for accomplishment of the voyage from land to land, being an average of 100 miles a day, which, all circumstances considered, is a fair progress for a canoe sailing half the time on a wind in the trades and the other half with variable winds and perhaps calms, the wind in that district of the ocean at that season (December) being, however, generally fair from the northward and eastward. We know that the voyage was made in December, because the pohu-tukawa (Christmas tree) was in bloom when the canoes arrived on the coast of New Zealand.

As for the canoes themselves, we may reasonably believe that they were like those used for hundreds of years after-wards by the descendants of their crews, and such as some persons still living have seen in New Zealand. Speaking generally, they were rather crank in build and dis-proportionately long for sea going pur-poses; but they could accommodate many rowers, and in smooth water were able to make good progress for a few miles by pulling. Their draught was too light for sailing close to the wind. They required to be about seven points off the wind to move through the water properly, which, with heave of the sea and drift when the sea was rough, would make a true course, say, of eight points, the course they would have to make in crossing the south-east

*The great labour of growing taro Maori caused it to be abandoned when the taro Merekena was introduced. The latter is hardy, prolific—runs wild. In fact—and easily culti-vated: but it is very inferior in flavour and flouriness to taro Maori. I don't think I have seen the taro Maori for thirty years. In the early forties a new kind of kumara (kumara Pakeha) was brought to New Zealand, which rapidly came into favour. It was more easily cultivated and made into kao than kumara Maori, and in about twenty years had super-seded it. I have not seen the kumara Maori for many years, perhaps twenty.

trades. Their lines were so fine that with a fair wind they sailed very quickly. One fault they all had, and that was leaking through the caulking of the top sides. This was due to the nature of the con-struction of the vessel, and was unavoid-able in the absence of ironwork attach-ments. The whole force of propulsion by sailing or pulling came upon the lashings that secured the top sides to the body of the canoe. This caused the seam to work a little, and baling was necessary from time to time when the canoe was deeply laden. If the lashings were sound, the fault was one of inconvenience, not of danger. It must, however, on the Hawaikian voyage, have entailed constant vigilance to keep their seed dry, which, if wet with salt water, would have been ruined.

Before the Hawaikians commenced their voyage, their anxiety was to prevent a separation of the canoes during the passage. They were all relations and friends, who were afraid, if once the ocean parted them, they would never see each other again. Therefore, at starting, some canoes were attached together, and progress was made in that manner while the weather remained fine; but that condition did not last. A change took place; a storm arose; the canoes were endangered by their nearness to each other, and the lashings of the attachments were cut one night by the crews to save themselves. When morning dawned, all the canoes had separated and lost sight of one another. After that, each canoe pursued its own lonely course, following independently the line of naviga-tion that had been determined upon before they left Hawaiki.

Thus, without compass, quadrant, or chart, of which they knew nothing, these ancient sailors possessed, nevertheless, in-trinsic qualities which helped them on their way. They were endowed with know-ledge, skill, forethought, resolution, and endurance. They knew the positions and movements of the heavenly bodies suffi-ciently well to be able to steer a course by them to the land they were bound for. Day after day, under skies for the most part clear, they observed the sun, noting his position at certain times, and they watched the direction of the winds and waves in relation to his course, and steered thereby. At night, the task of steering by the stars was easier. The motions of the moon and planets in the ecliptic showed the eastern and western points of the horizon, and the south (tonga) was always visible as the centre round which the Cross and Pointers revolved: and so each captain in his own canoe maintained his course, keeping, no doubt, if anything, a little to windward (i.e., southward) of it—prevailing winds, as I have said, in November and December being easterly—until he knew he had run his distance to the south, when he shaped a course to the westward and boldly ran down upon the land. That this was done is evidenced by the accuracy with which the land-fall was made at a certain parallel of latitude, and by the fact that the canoes Arawa and Tainui, that had overshot the mark, turned back northward when they reached the coast and rejoined their companions at Ahuahu, Mercury Island. The captain of a canoe, and each canoe had its captain, would know by celestial observation when he was far enough south. He could tell this by estimating, by a standard of some sort, the altitude of a polar star when nearest to the horizon; thus, for instance, he might hold to a southerly course until he had made the lowest star in the Cross rise above the horizon and be equal in altitude to half the altitude of the highest star in the same constellation at the time of their lower meridian passage, or he might have made other good observations, and that without a quadrant. The objection of the right ascension in a short summer's night has no force, as there are several large stars between 58° and 62° S. declination, and with large differences in R.A., and one or other of these he would be sure to catch.

The skill, tact, and ability of the old sailors who navigated their canoes from Hawaiki to New Zealand, so many canoes with such precision, is really wonderful. Could the certificated sailor of the present age have done better? Deprive him of his appliances, his compass, chronometer, and chart, his sextant and nautical almanac, and see then whether his intrinsic qualities would, on the same voyage, have enabled him to do better—especially if put into a long, lean, rather leaky, open boat, that had no draught, could he have sailed her better, have kept a perishable cargo better, or maintained better discipline amongst a numerous company of both sexes? There can be but one reply to these questions, namely, that under the same circumstances and conditions, it would be difficult even now to excel the old Hawaikian sailors in the execution of their craft.

The time of year at which the migration was made shows forethought. The line season had set in and the hurricane months had not begun, and there was still time on arrival in the new country to plant the seed they had with them; moreover, they would have several months of summer weather in which to explore and form settlements.

It is not my intention in this narrative to give all the movements of each canoe of the flotilla, or all the doings of the people of each after arrival. I shall simply mention

their names as they have been given to me and a few circumstances connected with some of them, and in noticing the others I would wish to treat of the movements of four of them more particularly, namely, Mataatua, Takitumu, Tainui, and Te Arawa, as the immigrants by these vessels settled in the districts with whose history I am best informed. The following are the names of the canoes:—Matawhaorua (which returned to Hawaiki), Arawa, Tainui, Mataatua, Takitumu, Kurahaupo, Aotea, Tokomaru, Mahuhu, Pungarangi, Rangimatoru and Whatu Ranganuku.

Te Arawa made land at Whangara, 18 miles north of Gisborne, but did not land there. From Whangara she coasted along to the north; off Whangaparaoa she spoke the Tainui coming in from the sea. The Arawas say that Tainui was then making her landfall. This some Tainui people contradict, stating that their canoe first made land at Te Mahia. The Arawa did not join Tainui, but continued her course, then shaping westward, and crossed the Bay of Plenty; and next we hear of her at Ahuahu, Mercury Island, where we will leave her for the present.

Whether Tainui made land at Te Mahia as her people say, or at Whangaparaoa as the Arawas affirm, is an open question. She was making for the shore when she passed the Arawa, and shortly afterwards she was nearly lost, and perhaps all on board, in a very simple and unexpected manner. At Cape Runaway there is a reef of detached rocks; there too is a perennial current that, setting strongly out of the Bay of Plenty, impinges against the Cape and reef. The Cape itself is a high headland studded with pohutukawa trees. As the canoe approached the Cape, in the bay round which a landing [was] proposed, the crew, whose attention was diverted to the beautiful bloom of the trees on the hillside, suddenly found themselves caught and carried swiftly towards the rocks by the current, of the existence of which neither they nor any stranger could have had a suspicion*, and because of the heavy rollers of the Rangawhenua† the danger appeared to be terrible. Here with a vengeance were

*The current at Cape Runaway is the tail race to a vast dam that Nature has placed across the course of part of the tropical off-flow of the South Pacific. The dam extends from the North Cape of New Zealand to Cape Runaway, or it may be to the East Cape. We are justified in believing that the stream comes from the tropics by its warm temperature, the fish, such as sharks, that frequent it, and by the tropical shells, like the nautilus, that are found on the shores adjacent.

†The Rangawhenua is an ocean swell that breaks heavily on the north-east coast of the North Island of New Zealand during the months of November, December and January. Along the beaches of the Bay of Plenty, fishing is stopped by it.

'the waves of the summer, as one died away another as sweet and as shining came on.' The wayworn voyagers, turning their eyes from the beautiful land, grasped the situation at a glance, and their hearts fell from the heights of joy and hope to the depths of fear. Were they after all their suffering and pilgrimage to be sacrificed at the gates of Paradise on those jagged rocks. Promptly the priest betook himself to his prayers, and quickly the crew plunged their paddles in the tide; but it was too late, before they could change their vessel's course she had struck sideways on a rock and remained there, the mussel shells grinding into her sides to the peril of her lashings; and now the danger of being dashed to pieces by the next wave or filling beside the rock, which is awash, is great indeed; fortunately, the rock was between them and the wave, for the current that pinned them to it ran against the swell. And then the very thing they feared became their friend. A roller broke upon the rock and its unimpeded portion circling quickly round the rock caught one end of the canoe, and raising it up flung it off wide from the rock. This was the moment of salvation; with a flash, before the current could push her back, all the paddles were buried for dear life in the seething foam, and Tainui, as if instinct with life, had shot into the open sea. The priest said they had been saved by the Atua to whom he had prayed, and his words were believed by those who heard him and by many succeeding generations. But the captain in going round the point again gave those rocks what sailors call a wide berth. Then the wearied people of Tainui rested at Whangaparaoa Bay and refreshed themselves; but the story that they found a dead whale on the beach in that bay and disputed with the Arawa about the possession of it is difficult to reconcile with the fact that the Arawa deny having gone there at all, and with the harder fact that dead whales not only don't drift into the bay, but cannot even be towed on to the shore there by several whaleboats after they are killed, the current above mentioned preventing it. There was a whaling station many years in Whangaparaoa Bay in the forties, and during that time the fish were 'tried out' at a place on the coast round the Cape, much to the inconvenience of the whalers, who at first often tried in vain to tow the dead whales into the Bay.

From Whangaparaoa the Tainui sailed along the shores of the Bay of Plenty, inspecting the country as she went. At Hawai a man named Taritorongo left her, and going inland joined the aborigines at Motu, as has been mentioned; also, we have seen how Torere left the Tainui, and how she was pursued by Rakataura, who,

failing to find his inamorata, returned and rejoined his companions at Kawhia. Rakataura landed at Tailiaruru, at Opape. When next we hear of Tainui she had arrived at Ahuahu, where the meeting of canoes took place. There is reason to assume from subsequent events that the Arawa and Tainui had made a comprehensive survey of the Bay of Plenty before they met at Ahuahu.

Up to this time there is not much to say about Takitumu further than to report that her landfall was made at the Great Barrier, and that passing Cuvier Island she had arrived at Ahuahu also.

Mataatua, though not in company with Takitumu, sighted the same land. She passed Cuvier, which was named Repanga by Muriwai, the chieftainess on board of her, in honor of her son, the young man who afterwards went to Kohipawa, and then the canoe sailed into Ahuahu Harbour.

At Ahuahu (Great Mercury) a conference took place between the captains of the canoes and other chiefs of the expedition, which resulted in the arrangement of the course, or line of action, that each canoe should take on leaving the island. Hence the name of the island, which is called Ahuahu to the present day, and is an abbreviation probably of Ahu te Ahu—to shape a course. I have never heard whether any of the other canoes were at this meeting; Pungarangi and Whatu Rangnuku could not, however, have been present, as they came to New Zealand afterwards.

I have referred several times to the captains, or nautical experts, of the canoes. The captain of Takitumu was Paikea; of Tainui, Hotunui; of Te Arawa, Tama te Kapua; and of Mataatua the captain was Toroa.

And now we view these and other chiefs, whose names have been handed down to posterity, at this the first Hawaiki Maori meeting held in New Zealand. There, too, we see seated upon the pebbly strand that forms the landing at Mercury Harbour, groups from the several canoes, all dressed in the tappa clothing of a tropical climate. They are assembled listening to their leaders, who are discussing the situation in its various aspects.

They have, indeed, found the country they sought, but exploration so far has shown it to be peopled with many tribes of aborigines resembling themselves and speaking their own language, of whom, notwithstanding their inoffensive behaviour, it behoves them to be aware. Apart from rugged coastlines, they have nowhere seen an unoccupied country large enough for them all to settle upon. They have but just escaped with labour and loss from internecine strife about land, where land was scarce and areas small. The horror of

what occurred then is fresh in their minds.
They cannot forget it, and, therefore, they
think they had better separate and incur
the risk of war with the aborigines to fighting amongst themselves ; besides, the
former risk appeared to be but small if a
policy of tact and forbearance were pursued
towards them, and that by and by when
they themselves had become numerous they
could disregard them.

Two rivers falling into the Bay of Plenty
had been discovered where settlement
would be possible, but more inviting districts might yet be found.

To one of these, however, the people of
Mataatua under Muriwai decide to go.
The other the leaders of Te Arawa have
determined to occupy should nothing more
suitable be found on further search.* The
immigrants in Tainui are of opinion that
in a country so large and promising
the chances are that they will secure a
better location by prosecuting their voyage
of discovery ; while those of Takitumu
resolve to search the Bay of Plenty for
themselves.

Such and similar were, doubtless, the
affairs that were considered at that meeting
—a meeting which heralded to New Zealand the birth of a new nation, who should
cultivate her soil and increase her civilisation, and whose warriors, orators, states-
men and priests, craftsmen and people of
low degree, were destined in the distant
future to supplant the more simple sons of
the soil almost throughout the whole country.

After the meeting the canoes left Ahuahu.
Tainui explored the Thames and found the
inhabitants numerous ; she passed from
there along the coast to the North, and
turning back again arrived at Tamaki
River, which was ascended, and then she
was dragged across the isthmus at Otahuhu
into Manukau, from which harbour she
put to sea, and, coasting southwards,
arrived at Kawhia. This was the end of
her voyage, for at Kawhia her people determined to settle.

Mataatua sailed from Ahuahu to Whakatane direct. Her unwavering course is
highly suggestive of information received,
either by Te Aratawhao (if that canoe
reached Hawaiki) or by Tainui, probably
the latter, for none of the people of Te
Aratawhao returned to Whakatane in
Mataatua. Ngatiawa found the country
at Whakatane unoccupied by the aborigines, and Kapu pa was empty. They

*The Arawa had most probably visited
Maketu and Tauranga on her voyage through
the Bay of Plenty, and had found the latter
thickly peopled, for on her return to those
parts she passed close by the mouth of Tauranga
Harbour in the daytime without entering it,
and went straight to Maketu. notwithstanding
the inviting aspect of the Tauranga country.

lived at first on the flat by the mouth of the
river, and there Muriwai died and was
buried, and her tomb under a rock there
can be seen at the present time. Toroa
went to Hokianga, at Ohiwa, to interview
Toi, who asked, ' Who are you, and where
do you come from ?'

To which Toroa replied, ' I am Toroa
(albatross) ; I have flown across the ocean
to this place.'

Toi then asked, ' Why have you come
here ?'

Toroa said, ' I have come to see and to
stay.'

Then food was set before Toroa, and
when he had eaten he returned to Whakatane.

This short conversation as it has been
handed down by tradition describes the
situation succinctly.

From Ahuahu the Arawa sailed to Cuvier
Island, where Hawaikian birds were re-
leased, and thence to the Great Barrier,
from which place she crossed over to Wha-
ngarei and coasted to Cape Brett ; there
she turned back and arrived at Tamaki, at
the head of which river she found Tainui,
whose crew were engaged laying the skids to
tow their vessel upon in crossing the isthmus.
The Arawa did not remain long at Otahuhu,
but sailed away to Moehau (Cape Colville),
for time was becoming precious.   Her
people landed at Moehau, but did not stay
there, notwithstanding Tamati Kapua was
so pleased with the place that he urged
them all to go no further, and to settle
down and make their home there.   From
Moehau they resumed their voyage, and
passing along the shores of the Bay of
Plenty, sailed straight to Maketu.   Thus
ended their long and toilsome voyage from
Hawaiki.

In passing Te Taroto, between Katikati
and Te Awanui (the ancient name of Tauranga entrance), Hei stood up and said,
' The land opposite to us,' pointing to Tauranga, ' is Te Takapu a Waitaha ' (the belly
of Waitaha), his son. Thus he bespoke the
Tauranga country, of which, however, he
and his son never got more than the
eastern end, which is a comparatively small
part of the district. The aboriginal inhabitants were too numerous to allow him
to take more. Off Wairakei, Tia stood
up and declared that the land at Rangiuru
and country adjacent was the Takapu of
his son Tapuika. In this manner he took
the land he had pointed out. Tamati
Kapua then thought it time to rise. He
took Maketu by calling that part of the
country Te Kureitanga o taku Ihu, shape of
his nose (end of his jib). The headland of
Maketu Point is still known by the name
of Okurei. Now, all this was a very solemn
and binding form of appropriation. No
one could interfere with the property after

that without trampling on the belly, etc., of the person named, and without being prepared to stand by his act in so doing.

The behaviour of those three men in greedily snapping up all the land in sight from the canoe before they had landed had the effect of compelling other members of the party to scatter in search of country, and thus the Ngaoho (or Arawa) tribe quickly spread into the interior as far as Taupo.

Takitumu, whose other name was Horouta, had the reputation of being a sacred canoe. It is said they took slaves on board at Hawaiki, whom they kept in the bow, and killed and ate from time to time as they required. This canoe left Ahuahu, and went to Tauranga, where they found they could not settle. The aborigines permitted a very few persons to remain, probably they hoped to profit by the Hawaikians' knowledge of agriculture. The canoe then continued her voyage, the next place she called at being Ohiwa, where she was nearly lost on Tuarae Kanawa shoal, at the mouth of the harbour. A few individuals were suffered to leave her here, who, as we have seen, became the progenitors of some of the present inhabitants in that part of New Zealand. Toi doubtless thought there were already enough Hawaikians in his neighbourhood at Whakatane, and perhaps Ngatiawa objected to the propinquity. Leaving Ohiwa the canoe Takitumu continued her search along the coast for a place of settlement, and as evidencing how fully the country must have been in the occupation of the aborigines at that time, I will enumerate a number of specially favourite residences of native tribes that were passed by the Hawaikians of Takitumu while searching for a place where they might safely make their future home : Opotiki, Te Kaha, Wharekahika, Kawakawa, including Horoera, Waiapu Valley, Tuparoa, Waipiro, Tokomaru, Tangoiro to Anaura, Uawa and Puatai—all these sites for settlement were passed before Paikea thrust his canoe ashore at Whangara, and declared the voyage to be finished. He named the place Whangara from a fancied resemblance to a place of that name at Hawaiki.

From the isthmus of Otahuhu northward the Hawaikian element in the population of Aotearoa was derived from the canoes Mahihi (or Mahuhu, as it is called in some parts of the country) and Kurahaupo.

The canoe Aotea landed on the West Coast at the place of that name. Her people travelled southwards, and occupied a wide area south of the Taranaki district.

Tokomaru canoe made the coast at Tokomaru, where the people who came in her landed, but did not remain. We hear of her next as having arrived at Mokau, on the West Coast, but whether she passed round the North Cape, or made the shorter cut by Tamaki and Manukau, seems to be uncertain. Her occupants were the forefathers of the Atiawa tribe at Waitara and Taranaki, from whom is descended a Ngatirahiri hapu ; just as the Ngatirahiri in the North are descended from the Ngatiawa progenitor who landed in Mataatua at Whakatane.

Pungarangi canoe made land at Rurima islets, in the Bay of Plenty; for some reason they were unable to land on the mainland, probably too heavy a sea was breaking on the coast, or the Tini o Taunu at Matata may have been hostile. The passengers had no water, and were greatly distressed by thirst. They landed in the little harbour at Rurima and rested, but were unable to find water, and all feared that a cruel death was before them. Then the chief of the party sought himself for water, trying in many places. At last he found a moist spot by the root of a pohutukawa tree, he dug a hole, and water trickled in and he drank, and the people drank and were saved. That little cup of water is there still, six centuries of time have not removed it, but the root is gone. As I looked at it I came to the conclusion that underground drainage had been arrested by the digging, and turned to the surface, where it has since remained. From Rurima the canoe went South to Wairarapa, and some of her people crossed Cook's Strait and settled at Nelson.

It will be remembered that the Arawa was unable to bring all the Ngaoho party, and that some were to follow in another canoe. The canoe they came from Hawaiki in was the Whatu Ranganuku. She landed them at Wairarapa, in a part where the inhabitants were hostile. The leader of the party, Tauwera, was ill-treated and badly burnt by them, so that he could not walk. The perpetrators of this outrage were not aborigines, but Hawaikians who had arrived there previously, and their object was not to kill, but to drive Ngaoho away. The latter took the hint, and left, carrying their disabled chief in a litter by the Kowhai road to the Bay of Plenty, and to the left bank of Waitahanui River at Te Takanga, where they settled, and this was the beginning of Waitaha Turauta tribe, or hapu of the Arawa, members of which, among the other Arawa sections, are still numerous.

The last canoe I have to mention is Rangimatoru. It is stated that she ended her voyage at Ohiwa. She is a canoe that has been very much lost sight of by the natives. Her reputation is eclipsed by that of Mataatua, close by at Whakatane, and of the existence of the representatives, if any, of her immigrants, or who her immigrants were, I have no proper information. The fact that the canoe came seems sufficiently established. Possibly the extinct Whakatane sprang from the people of that canoe. They were a tribe of Hawaikian extraction who owned the land between Ohiwa and Waiocka River inland, in the mountain region. The Upokorehe held the land in the north adjoining the possessions of the Whakatane. The former were destroyed, and the latter nearly so, by the Whakatohea. More than fifty years ago an old man of the name of Rangimatoru was a principal man of the remnant.

This concludes my account of the voyages of the canoes from Hawaiki to Aotearoa. I have, however, to add that Takitumu made a voyage from Whangara to Otago, where she remained, and is pointed out to the traveller of the present day, as she lies at her journey's end in the form of a rock. The Arawa made a voyage to Te Awa o te Atua and back. Then she was hauled up on the eastern bank near the entrance to Kaituna River, where she was burnt afterwards, and where a grove of ngaio trees grew down to the present generation, which trees were sacred to the memory of the old vessel.

In reviewing the movement from Hawaiki to New Zealand from a practical point, we are justified, if the foregoing statements and observations are accepted, in arriving at the following conclusions :—

That the Hawaikians emigrated under pressure arising out of troubles chiefly about land.

That as a necessary preliminary they explored the sea to discover a country where they might go.

That the exploration was successful, and was probably conducted upon an idea derived from tradition.

That the Hawaikians were skilful sailors, and notwithstanding the want of appliances they were good practical navigators by celestial observation. That as they had no means of finding the longitude on a true course, the same being a rhumb line, also as unknown currents and variable winds rendered the making of a true course impossible without the necessary aids, they devised the expedient of leaving the true course wide off on one hand, say a point or two, while making the required latitude (which they were probably able to find), having arrived at which they ran down the longitude. It was in this way I believe that eight canoes on a voyage of 1,500 or 2,000 miles (according to whether they came from Cook's Islands or the Society Islands) managed to make land on the East Coast of the North Island of New Zealand within 2½ degrees of latitude of each other. They all came straggling in singly, and four of them were within thirty miles of each other. There could have been nothing accidental about results so uniform; evidently the aid of science was invoked, roughly, no doubt, but sufficiently to serve all practical purposes.

That the Hawaikians introduced the art of cultivation into New Zealand, where they found an aboriginal race resembling themselves in appearance and speaking the same language.

That in selecting sites for settlement they avoided the localities that were thickly peopled by the aborigines, towards whom until they themselves had become numerous they behaved with much circumspection.

IT was many years ago, before our utilitarian grass paddocks and barbed-wire fences had changed the face of the country, that I first saw the picturesque ruins of old Tawhitirahi pa at Opotiki. Standing on a high cliff that overhangs the stream of Kukumoa they were embowered with trees and flowering plants that festooned from them to the stream below. The prospect from the pa was delightful; on the one hand far as the eye could reach the ocean and its coast lines were visible; on the other the valley of Opotiki was everywhere in view. The site, too, was as convenient as it was pleasant. Fishing in salt water and fresh, bird snaring and eel catching, were near to hand, while fern root in abundance of finest quality, and Tupakihi wine in the season were easily obtained. It was here some 350 years ago that a happy tribe lived of Maui-Maoris of Awa descent*; when they received a friendly visit from the chief of the powerful neighbouring tribe of Ngatiha, of the same descent (afterwards called Ngatipukenga), who lived at Waiaua and Omarumutu. The visitor greatly admired a tame tui, belonging to his host Kahukino, that sang and was otherwise well educated. In that age birds were taught to bewitch people, and to karakia (say prayers) for supplies of various kinds of food. When the visitor was about to return home he asked that the bird might be given to him, but Kahukino could not make up his mind to part with it. The visitor concealed his rage and went away. It was not long after this that Tawhitirahi pa was surprised one night by a war party with the late visitor at its head. The pa was taken, some of its chiefs and people were slain; many, however, escaped and fled to the forest-clad mountains of the interior, where they wandered for a time, but could not remain as they were trespassing on the hunting grounds of other tribes. Thus they passed through Motu country, and crossing its eastern water-shed, descended into the valley of the Waikohu, where they were found by the Takitumu natives of Turanganui (Poverty Bay), and would have been slain had not Waho o te Rangi interposed. He was the chief of Ngaeterangihokaia, a hapu of Te Aetanga Hauiti, of Takitumu descent, who lived at Uawa (Tologa Bay).

Waho o te Rangi, like Tuterangiwhiu at

Raukumara, took the refugees and made slaves of them. They were located on Te Whakaroa Mountain, inland of Waimata, and made to catch birds and carry them to him at Uawa.

At this time the people who laboured in this unhappy plight were known by the name of Te Rangihouhiri, being so called after their chief, who was the son of Kahukino, of Tawhitirahi. Kahukino was now an old man, and had ceased to take an active part in administering public affairs. Tutenaehe, the son of Rangihouhiri, grew up in this house of bondage.

In process of time Waho o te Rangi grew old and approached his end. The aged chief believed that there would be no one in the tribe when he was gone who would be capable of retaining possession of the slaves. He felt sure that another tribe by no means friendly to him would come and remove the slaves, thereby strengthening themselves and weakening his (Waho's) tribe. It was bad enough to be weakened, but worse that at the same time the other side should be strengthened. He chose the lesser evil, and determined to kill his slaves.

It happened by some means that the slaves learned the fate that was in store for them, and as even the worm will turn, so this poor people turned at bay, resolved to sell their lives dearly. Although their slaves had taken alarm and could not be surprised, the masters thought little of the task before them. Judge, then, their astonishment when their heedless onslaught was met by an organised band of skilled warriors, who killed them instead, and drove them back the way they had come. The Rangihouhiri had broken their bonds and never served again. They decided now to leave that part of the country, and seek elsewhere for a place where they might make a home for themselves, and marched towards the sea at Whangara, near which, on the banks of the Pakarae, they were attacked by the combined forces of Te Aetanga* Hauiti, the tribe of which their late masters were a section, whom they defeated a second time in a pitched battle, and remained masters of the field. Te Aetanga Hauiti now found that they must make terms. They had altogether mistaken the men whom they had been accustomed to despise, whose quality man for man was far superior to their own, whose prestige before the misfortune at Opotiki had been equal to their own, and whose spirit disciplined and elevated by adversity and self-sacrifice was unconquerable. They

---

* I would not imply that this tribe has not a strain of Hawaikian blood; no doubt it has, and like some others it knows more about its Hawaikian ancestors than its aboriginal lineage. This is due to causes I have already mentioned.

proposed that fighting should cease, and that Te Rangihouhiri should leave the district, going by canoes, which were to be prepared by both parties, and Te Rangihouhiri were to have time and opportunity to collect supplies of food for the journey. These proposals were accepted, they suited the Rangihouhiri perfectly, and both sides observed them faithfully. In due time the Rangihouhiri set sail, and steering north arrived in the Bay of Plenty, where they landed at a place called Hakuranni, and lived there.

Now, accounts conflict as to this locality. I will mention them, not because the site of that place affects our story, but just to illustrate practically how tradition, like history, varies sometimes in its facts. There are two Hakuranni pas at the Bay of Plenty, one south of Raukokore, the other at Torere. Ngaitai, of Torere, say Te Rangihouhiri never lived at their place, while the people of Raukokore say Te Rangihouhiri did live for a time at Hakuranni, that is upon their land. These statements, one would think, should be conclusive, but they are not, for the descendants of the Rangihouhiri aver that the Hakuranni in question is at Torere, and the Arawa who, as we shall presently see, have a voice in the matter, support the Rangihouhiri version.

However, no matter where it was, the location was not comfortable. The people of the district disapproved of their intrusion and harassed them; they had to keep close for stragglers did not return, and it was almost impossible to cultivate, as the following instance showed:—Two men of Te Rangihouhiri, Awatope and Tukoko, went out into a field to plant gourd seed. Awatope proposed to sow broadcast and get away for fear of the people of the place. Tukoke objected to such a slovenly method, and set to work to dibble his seed in properly. Awatope quickly sowed his broadcast and made off. His companion was busily engaged dribbling in, when he was suddenly caught and killed. It is true they made reprisals, but the place was not worth fighting for, and therefore they went away. Passing Opotiki and their old pa at Tawhitirahi, they came to Whakatane and built a pa for themselves on the spur of the hill that approaches the river next above Wainuitewhara. Here, on the strength of their military reputation, they lived undisturbed for a time. There was, however, sufficient uneasiness and uncertainty on all sides to make the chiefs of the Rangihouhiri think seriously of taking the initiative by a coup de main upon the Ngatiawa stronghold of Papaka (which position is immediately above the town of Whakatane). To this end Tamapahore, a leader of theirs, was one

night creeping about under the fortifications of Papaka looking out for a point of attack, when a woman came out of the pa on to the defences above him. She did not see him, but he saw her, and on the impulse of the moment he gave her a poke with the point of his taiaha. She raised an outcry, but Tamapahore escaped; the incident, however, betrayed the sinister designs of Te Rangihouhiri tribe. Moreover, the woman was the chief's daughter, and the insult was considered great by her tribe. All the Rangihouhiri knew at once that they must move on from Whakatane, and said so amongst themselves.

Then Tamapahore stood up and addressed them, saying: 'I have acted foolishly, and we must all leave this place in consequence, for all their hapus are roused, but we will not go meanly away; we will deliver a battle first, and then go.' The feelings of the people approved this sentiment, but Ngatiawa would have none of it, they were not going to fight for nothing. If Te Rangihouhiri stayed they would be wiped out; if they went at once they would be allowed to depart in peace. So the tribe of Te Rangihouhiri left Whakatane, and went to Te Awa o te Atua, where they were not wanted.

This friendless tribe had now wandered over the country 200 miles seeking a resting place, and no resting place could be found, for the land everywhere was occupied, or else claimed by someone. At that time Te Awa o te Atua was held by a section of Ngatiawa tribe, who not long before that had expelled the Tini o Tauru from the district. They did not intend that Te Rangihouhiri should remain with them too long, and by and by as the visitors manifested no intention of moving on, an intimation to go, too rude and realistic to be misapprehended, was given to them.

Then Rangihouhiri, the chief of the tribe of that name, sent Tamapahore on a friendly visit to Tatahau, the chief of Tapuika, at Maketu, and charged him to spy out the land there. Tamapahore went with a suitable retinue, and was hospitably received by Ongakohua, another chief of Tapuika. When he returned, Tamapahore reported that the place was most desirable in every respect. The aspect was pleasant, the land good, the cultivations beautiful, and fish of all kinds was abundant in the sea and rivers of Waihi and Kaituna, but the place was very populous, and Tatahau was a great chief, and closely connected with Waitaha a Hei, who were a powerful tribe also. However, the tempting character of the prize outweighed in Rangihouhiri's opinion all consideration of difficulty, and war with Tatahau was determined on, but a pretext was required to do the thing properly, and Rangihouhiri was too conscientious to misbehave, or act unjustifiably in the matter. Therefore, he applied to Tuwewea, the chief of Ngatiawa, at Te Awa o te Atua, who readily furnished the information required. Oddly enough, the *casus belli* took its rise out of the killing of their own man Tukoko, who, it will be remembered, had dibbled his seed instead of sowing broadcast, and that point being settled satisfactorily, preparation was made for the campaign, before entering on which I have a few general remarks to make.

We have seen that the Rangihouhiri tribe were Awa of Toi, that the tribe at Whakatane were Awa of Hawaiki, and that these two Awa tribes became connected by marriage and other causes, due to amicable propinquity, also by a portion of the latter (Te Kareke) being driven by civil war into the former and being absorbed by them. We may suppose that the force of these affinities was greater when proximate; operating as it were upon an inverse ratio to the square of their distance, and extended over a considerable area, including Tawhitirahi; and when in time the intervening connection consolidated, it broke up into tribes and hapus of aboriginal or immigrant appellation, according to the degree of relationship of each to one or other of the centres of settlement, the former being known as the Whakatohea hapus, the latter as Ngatiawa : but in the cases of Te Rangihouhiri of Tawhitirahi and Ngatirawharo of Ohiwa (both intimately connected together), the Awa of Toi have called themselves Ngatiawa, for they are related to Ngatiawa, and the more popular name has been adhered to by them.

It was in the summer time that the Rangihouhiri tribe set out from Te Awa o te Atua and marched towards Maketu. The main body camped at Pukehina under Rangihouhiri the chief, while a strong vanguard took up a position at the ford at Waihi, giving out that they were a fishing party. Presently ten men crossed Waihi and searching among the plantations on the hill above Maketu found a woman at work by herself collecting caterpillars off her kumara plants. She was Punoho, Tatahau's daughter. Her they outraged. The last of the party to approach was Werapinaki, a cripple. Filled with rage she derided his appearance, saying 'he would be a god if it were night time, in the day he is a hideous spectre,' when with a blow of his weapon he killed her, the body was thrown into a kumara pit where it could not be found. When Punoho was missed her tribe sought everywhere in vain, not a trace of her was seen. They suspected the Rangihouhiri of foul play, and sent a neutral woman to enquire. The answer the messenger received was ' Yes, she was

killed by Werapinaki.' Then a party of Tapuika stealthily crossed Waihi at night and slew Werapinaki, who was a chief, as he slept apart under an awning, the weather being hot, and next day the war began. The Rangihouhiri took the initiative by assaulting and carrying Tatahau's great pa at Pukemaire (where the old European redoubt stands). Tatahau and many of his tribe were killed, the rest and two of his sons escaped to Rangiuru. All the smaller pas followed the fate of Pukemaire. In this war the Rangihouhiri forces were materially strengthened by a section of their tribe that came from the Uriwera country, where it had taken refuge after the fall of Tawhitirahi.

Then the Ngaoho (Arawa) commenced a series of campaigns for the recovery of their lost territory and prestige. The first was by Waitaha a Hei, who came from East Tauranga, Tatahau's mother was of their tribe, and fought a battle, Te Kakaho, at Maketu ford and retired, for the weight of the Rangihouhiri arms was greater than they had expected. To mend this unsatisfactory state of affairs Tapuika strengthened themselves by matrimonial alliances with Ngatimaru at the Thames, and with the people at Maungakawa, from whom they got assistance in the next campaign. In the same way they tried without success to avail themselves of the help of the Hawaikian Awa, or Whanau Apanui, at Maraenui. On the other hand the Rangihouhiri summoned to their aid two Opotiki tribes, one of them (such is the irony of fate) was Ngatipukenga, who had commenced all their troubles by driving them out of their home at Tawhitirahi.

When ready the combined forces of Ngatimaru (Tainui) under Te Ruinga, Ranginui (Takitumu) under Kinonui, who was carried in a litter, also Waitaha and Tapuika under Tiritiri and Manu, sons of Tatahau, advanced upon Maketu. The first encounter was a night attack upon an outwork, Herekaki pa, which was taken and Tutenaehe the commander was slain. He was the eldest son of Te Rangihouhiri, who, when he heard the intelligence, exclaimed ' O ! my son you have gone by the night tide, I will follow by the morning tide !' He alluded to the tide because it is the custom in that part of the country, where much travelling is done by the beach, to wait for low tide to make a journey. Sure enough the old man's words came true, and by the morning tide he followed his son to the unknown world.

The next morning opened with the beginning of the battle of Poporohuamea, in which great numbers were engaged, and that lasted all day. The field of battle was on the high ground immediately above the entrance to Waihi River, and in the valley there that descends through the high ground towards the sea coast. It was there that the Maui Maori and the Hawaikian Maori joined issue in perhaps the greatest battle of the open field that was ever fought by the two races. The struggle ended at last in mutual exhaustion. The party in possession retired to its pas, and the other side, who had tried to oust them, gave up the attempt, re-crossed the Kaituna, and returned to the places they had come from. Te Rangihouhiri is the only great chief whose name is handed down as killed in this battle. From the death of Te Rangihouhiri the tribe of that name became known by the name of Ngaeterangi, by which name they are called at the present day.

After the battle of Poporohuamea the Ngaoho tribes (Arawa) of the lake district, took up the quarrel and determined to expel the intruding Ngaeterangi. Year after year they sent armies to Maketu not one of which made any impression on Ngaeterangi. The first army fought a little and returned home. The next was defeated with great slaughter at Kawa swamp, near Maketu, and their chief Taiwere was killed; that army returned to the lakes. Smarting under defeat and loss the Ngaoho again set forth to be again hurled back at Kawa with the loss of Moekaha, Taiwere's brother. They had as many killed at Kawa No. 2 battle as at Kawa No. 1. Assistance was now sought and obtained from Ngatihaua tribe, of the Upper Thames, and another campaign opened against Maketu, when a general action Kakaho No. 2 resulted in the crushing defeat of the combined Ngaoho and Ngatihaua. Haua, the chief of Ngatihaua, was slain, and Ariariterangi, the brother of Taiwere and Moekaha was drowned in making his escape. After this the Ngaoho, or Arawa, determined to avenge the death of Ariariterangi, and his son, Te Roro te Rangi, led an army against Maketu. This expedition effected nothing. After fighting awhile Roro te Rangi made peace with Ngaeterangi, offerings were given to cement the peace, and Roro te Rangi returned home to Rotorua.

Thus ended a war that had lasted many years, involving many tribes and much bloodshed, there had been several pitched battles in the field and the conquerors had stormed thirteen pas. Peace was made with the Tauranga tribes of Waitaha a Hei and Ngatiranginui (Waitaha Turauta on the east side of Maketu had taken no part in the war). As for Tapuika, their broken power was not worthy of consideration and was simply ignored. Ngaeterangi now held undisturbed possession of Maketu and about 75 square miles of excellent land, their territory extending half-

way to the lakes; with them were associated Ngatiwhakahinga, a co-tribe or section of Ngaeterangi, that had not been driven out of Opotiki by Ngatiha. Ngatipukenga (formerly called Ngatiha) returned to Waiaua after the battle of Poporohuamea, where they had suffered much; Ngaeterangi availed themselves of their assistance at the battle, but their presence was not particularly acceptable afterwards. We shall, however, hear more of this most pugnacious tribe, which, as it had rendered others homeless, by a just retribution became homeless itself.

Such was the peaceful condition of the political horizon to Ngaeterangi, as resting on their laurels they enjoyed the tranquil outlook, when suddenly another war-cloud rose of aspect most terrible; they were precipitated into it and all was strife again.

It happened that a canoe went out from Tauranga to fish in the open sea. Two chiefs were in this canoe, named Tauraweheke and Te Turanganui. A westerly gale arose and drove the canoe before it until it was lost and the people all drowned excepting one man, Tauraweheke, who escaped by swimming to Okurei, Maketu Point. Here he was found in an exhausted state by a woman who was looking for shellfish amongst the rocks. She took him to a sheltered place under the cliffs and went to fetch food and clothes for him. On the way she met her husband and told him how she had found Tauraweheke and where she had left him. As soon as she had departed on her errand the husband went and killed Tauraweheke and ate of him, and continued thus to indulge himself from time to time secretly, the people of his tribe, Ngaeterangi, knowing nothing about it, but his wife knew.

At Tauranga it was supposed that the canoe had been lost at sea with all hands. Sometime, however, after this, the man, evidently a brutal fellow, beat his wife severely, and she exclaimed, 'O! I can punish you by telling what you did.' The busy-bodies of the tribe (of whom there always is, have been, and will be a number everywhere) now sought to penetrate the mystery of the wife's words, nor stopped until the murder was out, and all over the place, and news of it had been taken to Tauranga. Ngatiranginui and Waitaha were not slow to seek revenge. They caught two Ngaeterangi chiefs at Otaiparia at Te Tumu getting toetoe. They were Tuwhiwhia and his son, Tauaiti. The father they killed, and putting his headless body into his canoe sent it adrift to float down the stream to Maketu. The son they took to Tauranga and killed at their leisure by torture and mutilation. In his agony Tauaiti said to his persecutors 'My pain is shallow compared to the ocean of pain to come,' signifying, thereby, what their pain would be like before long.

The drift canoe was seen at Maketu and told its own tale. Intelligence, too, of Tauaiti's suffering and death was subsequently received, and entered deeply into the feelings of the people. Their rage at the Tauranga people was dreadful, to whom they determined that the cup of wrath should be administered and drunk to the dregs. Then was seen how Kotorerua, the younger brother of Tauaiti, rose to the occasion. Putangimaru, a chief of Rankawa, at Waikato, was travelling at this time and came to Maketu ; he was known to be a wise man and powerfully possessed of the art of divination. Kotorerua suggested to his sister, Tuwera, that she should be complacent to their guest. Putangi was pleased and Tuwera returned with him to his home as his wife, and Kotorerua was invited to follow them to their place at Himuera in order that Putangi and he might have opportunity to divine and make plans together.

To avoid his enemies at Tauranga, Kotorerua travelled through the forest by Otawa to Te Pawhakahorohoro, where he found a guide left for him by Putangimaru named Ika. They travelled to Whennakura, whence all the country could be seen around. Ika pointed out the road and the place where Putangimaru lived. Kotorerua having got this information, killed Ika unawares, because he wanted some portions of his body to divine with before he met Putangimaru. Having performed this office, he pursued his journey, taking Ika's head with him. Putangimaru received Kotorerua with distinction, and asked if he had seen Ika. ' Yes,' said Kotorerua ; ' he brought me through the forest, and then I was able to find my way by myself ; so I killed Ika, as I had to divine before I met you.'

' You acted very wisely,' said Putangi.

' I have brought Ika's head for us both to divine upon,' said Kotorerua. This also received the approval of Putangimaru. Then they divined carefully and found the auguries favourable, and they took counsel together and formed the plan of a campaign. This done, Kotorerua returned to Maketu to push his preparations, and in due time he attacked the large pa of Ranginui and Waitaha at Maunganui.

The pa of Maunganui, situated on the hill of that name, covered about 100 acres. The fortifications crossed the top of the hill and ran down each side, then, circling round the base towards the south, they met. Waitaha held the east side and Ngatiranginui the west side of the pa, which enjoyed a beautiful view and splendid position on the shore of the harbour. The fortifications were so

strong and the garrison so numerous that the pa seemed impregnable to Maori weapons—no matter what the prowess, the situation, with the means at command, was unassailable. It was to take this pa that Putangimaru and Kotorerua had devised a plan as daring as it was able, and, perhaps, the only one by which the object could have been effected. On the top of the hill on the north side of the pa, there was a point 850 feet above the sea, which, under certain circumstances, would be vulnerable. Kotorerua undertook to solve the problem by inducing the required conditions and making the attack at that point, a narrow pass, flanked by walls of rock, and to which the approach from below, for an attacking party, was exceedingly steep. That point once secured, the pa must fall, for it was the key to the position. A handful of defenders, however, could hold it against any number from without. Kotorerua's scheme was to show no intention of making war on Kinonui, the chief of Maunganni ; on the contrary, he would lull suspicion by appearing to conciliate him with a handsome present. The offering should come to Kino late on the evening of a dark and stormy night. Kino and his people would then be occupied fully in entertaining the present-bearers, or pretending to entertain them, and in counselling amongst themselves and trying to fathom this new and unexpected departure by Kotorerua. In this way, many hours, perhaps the whole night, must elapse before Kinonui and his people would think of taking action of any kind, and during these precious moments of irresolution Kotorerua intended to destroy him ; for, meanwhile, under cover of darkness and storm, the whole force of Ngaeterangi would be thrown into the pa through the gap on the top of the hill. The army to perform this service would have to risk the storm in canoes, passing along the coast unseen at night, and landing immediately below the gap in a narrow channel between the rocks called Te Awaiti. The bearers of the present were to slip out of the pa in the darkness and cut the lashings of the topsides of all the canoes on the beach and rocks in front of the pa. If all went well, this rather complicated scheme would no doubt realise the hopes of its authors, but there were obviously several awkward contingencies connected with it, which must have caused considerable anxiety at the time to those charged with its execution. It happened, however, that everything came to pass exactly as Putangimaru and Kotorerua had planned.

One evening, Kotorerua and one hundred and forty followers, armed, presented themselves unexpectedly before the fortifications of Maunganui, bearing a present to

Kinonui of one hundred baskets of kokowai (red ochre); it was houru, the kind prepared by burning, and, it was said, had been obtained with much labour from the streams of Kaikokopu. The rain had overtaken them on the road, and they explained that they had been delayed while preventing their kokowai from getting wet. As it was too late to go through the formalities of presentation, the baskets were stacked at the quarters assigned to the visitors. Thus an inspection of the present was avoided, which was just as well, seeing that each was only a basket of earth, with a layer of kokowai at the top. Kotorerua and such of his followers as he desired to accompany him were taken to the large meeting-house in the pa, where the distinguished men of the pa met them. This large house, belonging to Kinonui, stood on the little plateau above the place that is now called Stony Point: and then ensued between the host and his guest a scene, sustained for hours, of courtly urbanity and matchless dissimulation, covering a substratum of deadly hate; each with unparalleled ability was playing for the almost immediate destruction of the other and of all who were with him. On the one hand, Kotorerua had to appear at ease and without a trace of anxiety, conversing about anything or nothing, to gain time and disarm suspicion—and this, notwithstanding his men might be discovered at any moment tampering with the canoes on the beach below the pa, and notwithstanding the safety of all concerned, and the success of the enterprise, depended upon the arrival in time of the canoes through the storm. On the other hand, Kinonui had at all hazards to keep his guest interested until daylight, when his people would be able to see what they were doing, for it was intended that Kotorerua and all his party should then be killed; they could not kill them in the night without accident and confusion, and some might escape in the darkness. Meanwhile, Kotorerua was not to be allowed to rejoin his men; but to kill him now would alarm them, and many would try to escape, therefore, the conversation was kept up between these two great actors, each working for his own ends, as they sat facing one another with apparent indifference, but watchful of every movement. Now and then an attendant of one of the chiefs would come in or go out, seemingly about nothing in particular, but really keeping communication open with their respective parties outside.

At length, Kotorerua was made aware that his time for action had arrived. All his staff had left the meeting-house as if fatigued; presently one of them returned about something and went out again,

leaving the door open after him. Kotorerua rose, and in a moment had passed swiftly out. Kinonui had not time to prevent him, so unexpected was the movement of the younger man and so sudden; he called after Kotorerua and ran to stop him, but it was too late, the sliding door was slammed in his face and the lanyard fastened outside. The time for mock ceremony has passed, that which is real must now take place. A torch is handed to Kotorerua and quickly applied to the raupo wall, the meeting-house is wreathed in flames, and Kinonui with his associates are immolated at the ceremony of their own funeral pyre.

Then, by the illumination cast around, an avalanche of war was seen descending from the mountain-top, sweeping its course right down to the sea, and crushing the people as it rolled over them. Such as escaped the dread invasion fled to their canoes and thrust off into the harbour, but the canoes, already wrecked, quickly filled with water, and the occupants were drowned in trying to swim to the opposite and distant shore.

Thus, with the head rather than the arm, did Kotorerua break the power of Ngatiranginui and Waitaha, and it was all done by a *coup de main* in a few short hours. The conquest of the rest of the district of Tauranga speedily followed. Katikati and the islands on the north side of the harbour were first subdued. This was Kinonui's own domain, and the poor people in it were too panic-stricken to offer any effectual resistance. Tamapahore took the Waitaha country on the east, including the possessions of the Kaponga, hapu of Ngatiranginui, at Waimapu, but the lands of the hapus of Kuraroa, between Waimapu and Wairoa, and Ruinga, between Wairoa and Waipapa, were still intact when Kotorerua returned to Tauranga after a temporary absence. He was then surprised and displeased to find that terms of peace had been granted to Ngatiranginui at Otumoetai pa, and that the same had been ratified by a marriage. Kotorerua refused absolutely to be a party to the arrangement, and he immediately attacked Otumoetai and destroyed the people in the pa. This, with the fall of some minor pas on the south side of the harbour, completed the subjugation of the Tauranga country by Ngaeterangi.

Kotorerua's campaign of Maunganui denotes consummate generalship, with troops of the finest quality and discipline, and a high military and naval organisation. Only with such material could such a daring and complicated scheme have been carried out, but the General knew the quality of his men, and therein he showed his capacity. The maxim, that for desperate cases desperate remedies are necessary, must, I suppose, be taken as a sufficient warrant for the General when staking everything upon the unknown quantity of a gale of wind at sea, but the auguries had been favourable, and we cannot tell how much that influenced him. I have myself been impressed with the unquestioning faith the old Maori chiefs had in the auguries vouchsafed to them. I remember such an one who went through many battles in the belief that no bullet could harm him. He might be wounded, he said (experience showed that), but he could not be killed. He died in his bed, with a reputation that extended throughout the North Island.

Wolfe, going by boat, took the enemy in rear at night on the Heights of Abraham, but he had not a sea voyage by boat in storm, and a night landing through breakers on the coast, to make. On the contrary, he had a river so calm to go upon that, we are told, he recited Gray's 'Elegy' to his staff at that time; nor had he to enter the enemy's camp and delude him, while in the act of destroying his means of retreat, by breaking his boats not one hundred yards away. Yet there was a rift in Kotorerua's lute which well nigh spoilt the harmony of his combinations. He was a young man, and his uncle, Tamapahore, was a veteran leader in battles. On this occasion, the latter, with his division, held aloof and did not join the flotilla, which was kept waiting for hours, until the very last moment possible, when at length he put in an appearance. This happened presumably through jealousy; however, pressure or loyalty to Ngaeterangi prevailed in the end, but Tamapahore never got a quarter in the pa at Maunganui. The place he chose was made too uncomfortable for occupation; the other Ngaeterangi rolled great stones down the hill into his location; he took the hint, and made a pa elsewhere at Maungatapu. The jealousy, if such, of this old Maori warrior was natural enough; more highly civilised soldiers have felt the same, and some have not come out of the ordeal as well. Witness, for instance, the misconduct of that Imperial Archduke, who, by withholding his hand, caused his brother to lose the field of Wagram. The Waitaha remnant fled to Te Rotoiti; the remnant of Ngatiranginui, as already stated, escaped into the forest at the back of Tepuna, and there they became known as Te Pirirakau, which is their name still.

It will be remembered how the aborigines permitted a few of the immigrants by Takitumu to settle at Tauranga; those persons kept up a connection with their compatriots at Whangara. Kahungungu, the ancestor of the great tribe of that name, was a Takitumuan of Tauranga, who left his native place and went south to live amongst the other Takitumuans because his elder brother had grossly insulted him, by striking him on the mouth with a kahawai (a fish). Similarly, two hundred and forty years after the settlement at Whangara had been made, Ranginui moved with his people from Hangaroa (between Poverty Bay and Wairoa, H.B.) to Tauranga, and camped on the left bank of the Wairoa, near where the bridge on the Katikati road is now. They were squatting on land belonging to Ngamarama, a numerous tribe, who owned the whole country west of Waimapu River. The Ngamarama resented the encroachment, and, to put a stop to it, caused two Ngatiranginui children to be drowned by their own children while bathing together in the Wairoa. The Ranginui children fled home and told what had been done to them. The tribe considered the matter, and next day the children were directed to return and bathe as though nothing had happened, and when the Ngamarama children joined them they were without fail to drown some of them; this the children did, and reported that they had drowned a Rangatira girl. War followed, resulting in time in the destruction and expatriation of Ngamarama, and this is how Ngatiranginui became possessed of Tauranga, where they lived undisturbed one hundred and twenty years, until Ngaeterangi came and took it from them, about two hundred and forty years ago.[*]

THE NGATIPUKENGA TRIBE.

I WILL now mention Ngatipukenga more particularly, who formerly lived at Waiaua, east of Opotiki, and were called Ngatiha. We have seen that they drove the Rangihouhiri away from Tawhitirahi, also that when the same Rangihouhiri took Maketu and killed Tatahau they, the Ngatipukenga, came to Maketu, hoping to join in the spoil, and took part at the battle of Poporohuamea. Their chiefs at that battle were Kahukino and Te Tini o Awa. The tribe, I should say, was of the ancient aboriginal stock. At the battle named they suffered severely, and recrossed the Waihi, whence they returned home. The Rangihouhiri had not forgotten Tawhitirahi and did not solicit their aid at the campaign of Maunganui. When they heard, however, of Kotorerua's success at at Maunganui, they hurried up to Tauranga to try and share in the spoil, and this time

*In the story of Te Waharoa, written twenty-nine years ago, though not published until the year following, I have placed the conquest of Tauranga by Ngaeterangi at 'about one hundred and fifty years ago.' My unit then for a generation was twenty years. My unit now is thirty years. Moreover, that was written one generation ago.

they managed to get a large tract of land next to Tamapahore's selection on the west side. Here they became so overbearing that all the Ngaeterangi hapus united against them about one hundred years ago, and drove them all completely out of the Tauranga district. At their rout they fled by way of Whareroa (where they left their canoes thickly lining the beach, which ever after was called Whakapaewaka) to Orangimate pa, half way to Maketu. Thus the measure meted by them to Te Rangihouhiri was measured to them by Ngaeterangi, Rangihouhiri's descendants.

After this expulsion Ngatipukenga hated Ngaeterangi bitterly, and never lost an opportunity of joining the enemies of that tribe.

When Tapuika fell before Ngaeterangi at Te Karaka, Ngatipukenga came and helped them to obtain revenge at Te Kakaho.

When Ngatiwhakahinga retired from Maketu before Ngatemaru, Ngatipukenga went and occupied that place.

Then Te Rarau from Waikato and Ngaeterangi attacked them, seeking to drive them away from Maketu, but effected nothing.

Then Ngapuhi, armed with guns, came, at whose approach Ngatipukenga fled inland to Te Whakatangaroa, near Te Hiapo, and Maketu was evacuated by them. But some time after Ngatitematera, from Hauraki, attacked and took Te Whakatangaroa, and Ngatipukenga fled to the lakes.

A war party of Ngatirawharo, allies of Ngaeterangi, going from Tauranga to attack Okahu pa at Rotoiti, were encountered enroute by Ngatipukenga, and an action was fought at Te Papanui, where Ngatipukenga were defeated.

After this the elder Taipari, of Hauraki, made peace with Ngatipukenga.

Ngapuhi came a second time to Tauranga, and on this occasion joined Ngaeterangi against Ngatipukenga, Orangimate pa was taken with much slaughter, and the refugees fled to Rotorua. At length Ngatipukenga decided to go to Hauraki, whence their feud could be carried on more easily and effectively. They, therefore, left Orangimate and Maketu, to which places they had returned from the lakes, and joined Ngatimaru at the Thames, by whom some of them were located at Manaia, near Coromandel, where they are now known as Te Tawera.

From the Thames they went with Ngatimaru to Maungatautari, from whence they operated against Ngaeterangi thrice, losing two engagements at Te Taumata and gaining one, in which the Ngaeterangi chief, Tarakiteawa, was killed.

Then followed the taking of Te Papa pa at Tauranga by Te Rohu, of the Thames, where Ngatipukenga were present and joined in the assault. Te Papa was destroyed in utu for the murder by Ngaeterangi of Te Hiwi, near the Wairoa River. Te Hiwi was a chief of Ngatiraukawa.

From Te Papa Te Rohu advanced to Maketu, Ngatipukenga accompanying him. They found the pa occupied by Ngapotiki of Ngaeterangi. The pa was taken and many Ngapotiki were slain.

Again Ngatipukenga followed Ngatimaru through the war at Haowhenua and Taumatawiwi, and after the defeat suffered there Ngatipukenga fled to Rotorua, where they hardly escaped death because they had murdered Te Kuiti at Rotorua, on a former visit, and because they had killed Te Oneone at Maketu. These were very good reasons why they should be killed and eaten, but they were saved through an old marriage of one of their chiefs with a Ngaitwhakane woman of rank. However, Ngatiwhakane would not allow them to remain at Ohinemutu, and they passed on to Maketu, which place they held until Te Waharoa took their pa and killed nearly the whole of them. The remnant fled back to Rotorua. When Maketu was re-taken by the Arawa this remnant returned to Maketu, where it has remained to the present time.

During the civil war at Tauranga in the fifties Ngatipukenga were invited from Manaia to help Ngatihe, with the promise of receiving land at Ngapeke, at Tauranga. They came and got the land, but rendered no military service for it, for the war was over before they arrived. A number of Ngatipukenga live at Ngapeke still.

The little tui was the ruin of Ngatipukenga. It involved them in a long struggle with Ngaeterangi that lasted for generations, and reduced their number to such an extent that they ceased to have power to disturb anyone; moreover they lost all their lands at Opotiki and Tauranga through the restless and pugnacious spirit which followed their adventure at Tawhitirahi.

NGATIRAWHARO TRIBE.

Ngatirawharo were like Ngaeterangi, only more Hawaikian, perhaps. Originally they lived at Ohiwa, whence they moved to Waiohau, on the Rangitaiki River. The Ngatipukeko, a tribe of Ngatiawa, objected to what they considered a trespass on their land, and attacked them. Marupuku was the chief of Ngatipukeko, who led this war, in which there was much fighting, lasting a long time. The following battles were fought: Whakaaronga, where Ngatirawharo suffered severely; then Putahinui and Pounatehe were engagements at which Irawharo were beaten and driven many miles toward the sea. This happened about the time that Te Rangihouhiri made their progress from Opotiki to Tauranga. Ngatipukeko continued from time to time, with more or less success, to wage war. They fought at Otamarakau at Waiohau, at Tamahanga near Raerua, at Tapuae, and at Omataroa. On each occasion they improved their position, and after the action last named Ngatirawharo were compelled to move off their land and cross the river at Te Teko ; but the people at Te Teko would not allow them to remain there, so they had no option but to move on, nor stopped until, with reduced numbers, they arrived at Otamarakau at Waitahanui. There, and at Te Ruataniwha, they settled, and remained a long time. At length they joined their friends, the Ngaeterangi, at Tauranga, where they have lived ever since. This tribe has forgotten that it has aboriginal blood in its veins.

THE WAR OF NGATIPUKEKO OF MATAATUA WITH NGATIMANAWA OF TE ARAWA.

Shortly after the termination of their war with the Kareke tribe at Te Poroa, Ngatipukeko, under Te Muinga, went to Te Whaiti to live. Te Muinga's example was not immediately followed by all the chiefs, but in the course of four or five years all the great chiefs had moved from Whakatane to Te Whaiti, Tehe only remaining at Papaka to take care of that place (Papaka, it will be remembered, was the strong pa at Whakatane that Tamapahore was prowling round on the night, when he grossly insulted a chief's daughter). In time about six hundred fighting men had settled at Te Whaiti, whose chiefs were Kihi, Mokai, Tautari in his youth, Te Mahuhu, and Te Moeroa. Their principal pa was Nihowhati. It happened one day that Tamahi of theirs set out on a journey to Whakatane, for numbers of the tribe continually passed and repassed between the two places. When he arrived at Puketapu, a pa at Mangahouhi, Tamahi met a war party of the Uriwera, under Puiteraagi, who slew him. Ngatihaka saw the deed and took the body of Tamahi and buried it. Soon after, three men of Ngatimanawa passing by, dug up the body and ate it. They were Manakore, Tarewarua, and Matarehua. When Ngatipukeko heard of it, all the body had been consumed.

Then Kihi led Ngatipukeko away from the members of all other tribes to a remote place in the forest, where he said he wished a clearing to be made, but when they had arrived on the ground he cast aside his stone axe and grasped his weapon, they all did the same, and a council of war was held to know what should be done. It was unanimously decided to avenge the insult offered by Ngatimanawa, and this was done by making a night attack under Kihi on Parakakariki pa, near Tutu Tarata. They killed Te Matau and vindicated their honour. Then peace was ostensibly made, and hostilities ceased.

After the foregoing episode messages came to Ngatipukeko at Te Whaiti, from the tribes at Taupo and Whanganui, asking them to come and fight for them. The tribe was summoned to a council of war, and Kihi urged the enterprise, saying to the chiefs Matua and Taimimiti : ' Go and lead the fight.' They answered : ' No, go you and lead, for you are our fighting chief.' (Kihi was probably afraid to leave the home of the tribe in the care of the two chiefs named.) However, he went with a war party of seven score men, and had a very successful campaign, taking pas at Whangaehu, near Whanganui.

During Kihi's absence Matua and Taimimiti went away on a fishing excursion (but Ngatimanawa chose to say they went to kill men in utu for the violation of Te Wharekohuru, Tautari's daughter). They were busy catching eels when they received an invitation from Ngatimanawa, at Wairohia near by. They accepted the proffered hospitality, and, as a reward for their simplicity, they and their party of seven were slain. Having thus committed themselves, Ngatimanawa immediately arose and destroyed two Ngatipukeko villages, Ngatahuna and another ; only one person escaped, who fled from the latter to Nihowhati. But though warned, Nihowhati was nevertheless destroyed, the bulk of the people being away. Te Muinga and one hundred people were burnt at Nihowhati in a large house in the pa, called Te Umu ki te Ngaere.

It happened, however, that one man, named Mato, escaped unperceived from the rear of the house, and gave the alarm to the scattered Ngatipukeko in the surrounding country, who all collected at Oromaitaki, where they were joined by the refugees of Ngatiwhare, for Ngatiwhare had suffered also, and there they built a pa to defend themselves. Karia was sent to recall Kihi, and fortunately met him returning with his war party close at hand at Kaingaroa.

On hearing the dreadful intelligence, the warriors of the Ngatipukeko whose families had been massacred, determined to kill Kihi on the spot for taking them away to Whanganui. But Kihi said : ' Let me live to get vengeance. If the other chiefs had lived you might have killed me, and I would have been willing to die, but they are all slain, and there is no one else to lead you now. Let me live to seek vengeance. Then Ngatipukeko spared him.

Soon they came upon a bird-catcher of Ngatimanawa, whom they questioned, and learned that they were close to the main body of Ngatimanawa, seven or eight hundred strong, who were about to attack Oromaitaki. Killing the bird-catcher, they advanced, and presently perceived the enemy reconnoitring the pa. They remained unperceived, and at daylight next morning attacked him unawares, routing him with slaughter and the loss of two chiefs; but they found at the end of the action that the bird-catcher had deceived them, and that the main body of the enemy had not been engaged. On this they became very cautious, watching all detached parties and cutting them off. By this means several score of Ngatimanawa were killed. At length a general action was fought, in which Ngatimanawa, although assisted by Ngatihineuru from Runanga, were defeated. Then for the first time Kihi's war party went to Oromaitaki to mingle their lamentations with the people there for the many murdered members of the tribe. For a short time only did they weep, and then they went out from the pa the same day to fight the enemy at Okarea. This was not a decisive action, but the next battle fought at Mangatara was entirely favourable to Ngatipukeko. It was a very peculiar battle, because it was fought by women. There were only thirty-seven Ngatipukeko men engaged, all the rest who fought were women, and the odds against them were fearful. But first, I should say that the Ngatipukeko army had been out-generaled. They were scattered in pursuit of detached parties, when suddenly Ngatimanawa fell, with concentrated force, upon their head quarters, where their families were. The women were equal to the occasion. They rigged up guys so well that the enemy was deceived, and in forming for attack laid himself open to an irresistible onset in flank. The Amazons displayed a wonderful courage and knowledge of the art of war. With hair cropped short and bodies nude* they charged into the undefended side of the enemy with such force as to throw him into confusion. Moenga was the distinguished Amazon of the day. She fought with a paiaka, and hewed the Ngatimanawa down on every side. On all sides the enemy fell, until he broke and fled ; the main body of Ngatipukeko army came up in time to follow in pursuit, nor stopped until Runanga was reached. From

*In Maori warfare it was absolutely necessary to fight naked, and with short hair, in order to give the enemy no means of catching hold of the body : for the same reason oil or fat, when obtainable, was smeared over the body before going into action.

there the Ngatimanawa, or rather, what were left of them, passed on to Mohaka, where Te Kahu o te Rangi, a chief of Ngatikahungungu, made slaves of them. Te Kahu soon found that he was being cheated by his slaves. The birds they caught were given to the chief of another tribe. Finding they were not to be trusted, he ill-treated and killed them.

Then Ngaetuhoe, a tribe of the Uriwera, took compassion on the miserable remnant of Ngatimanawa, and brought them away to Maungapohatu, and they had some old kumara pits given them to live in. While they lived in this abject condition at Maungapohatu, the Ngatimanawa sent Kato and others to Kihi to sue for peace. Their petition was granted, and terms were fixed. The next day another section of Ngatipukeko sent for Kato and his friends to hear and discuss the terms named ; this, however, was only a ruse, for, as soon as Kato and his companions appeared, some of whom were related to Ngatiwhare, they killed and ate them. Therefore, for ever after that treacherous hapu of Ngatipukeko was called Ngatikohuru (hapu of murderers).

Now, when Ngatipukeko had conquered Ngatimanawa, Ngatiwhare became afraid at their inflamed and blood-thirsty demeanour, and quietly withdrew to the mountains, and there remained, until intelligence was received of the murder of their friends by Ngatikohuru. Then, from being friendly from a distance, they changed and became active enemies to Ngatipukeko, although closely related to them, and revenge in some way was determined upon. The opportunity was not long in coming. News was received that Ngatipukeko were sending a deputation of chiefs to the Uriwera at Ruatahuna; instantly Ngatiwhare dispatched Karia, their chief, to Ruatahuna, there to persuade the Uriwera chief, Rangikawhetu, to kill the deputation when it should arrive. Rangikawhetu assented to Karia's proposal, and tried to carry it out. His success was only partial, for Mokai and Kuraroa escaped. This affair created a further complication in the political outlook, and for a long time Ngatipukeko were embroiled with the Uriwera tribe.

At this time Ngatipukeko had possession of the right bank of Rangitaiki from Waiohau to Te Whaiti, where they lived many years undisturbed, and then they returned under Kihi to Whakatane. From Whakatane they went to Te Awa o te Atua and lived a while, and there they saw Captain Cook's ship pass by. They went off to the vessel and saw the people on board of her. Again they returned to Whakatane, where a deputation from Ngatimanawa and Ngatiwhare sued for peace and to be permitted to return to their homes at Te Whaiti, and Ngatipukeko allowed them to go there.

A MAORI DUEL.

WHEN the Chief Matua was murdered, as I have said, while eel-catching at Waiirohia, he left a little son named Tama te Rangi, who grew up to be a man imbued with the strongest hatred of his father's murderers. This feeling had been carefully instilled into him by his widowed mother from earliest childhood, by songs and hakas, and by the persistent character of remarks which were specially directed against Potaua, and she took care to have Tama te Rangi thoroughly trained to the use of arms.

Potaua heard what the widow had done, and he feared to approach Te Tirina country, where she lived. At length he came to Puketapu, a pa on the Rangitaiki, by the racecourse at Te Teko. He was encouraged to venture there by the presence of Harehare and two other chiefs, with whom he thought he should be safe from insult and attack.

Tama te Rangi heard that Potaua had come to Puketapu in the Pahipoto country, and when he heard it he said to his people at Whakatane that he would go and see him.

Taking two companions he went, and at night he camped in the fern a mile or two from Puketapu pa. He informed the chiefs of the pa by a messenger that he had come, and they invited him to the pa for the night.

Tama te Rangi replied that they would see him come into their pa by the light of day.

The next morning Tama was seen approaching, and the whole population turned out to see what he would do. He came and walked up the narrow roadway into the public place of the pa, all people respectfully making way for him and his companions. Here on an arena already formed and guarded stood Potaua. The chiefs of the pa were standing at the further end of the space, beyond Potaua. Tama te Rangi entered the arena at once, and advanced confidently upon his enemy, who had a presentiment that his hour had come. This unnerved him, and the young man's vigour and skill overcame him, and he fell, slain by the avenger of blood, in the presence of all the people.

Hatua, the father of the late Rangitukehu, leaped forward, and by his great influence saved the other Ngatimanawa visitors, who in the excitement of the moment would have been killed on the spot by the people of his tribe.

ANOTHER MAORI DUEL.

It was in the lake country that Eke, a faithless fair, eloped to the forest with Utu,

a middle-aged chief of considerable authority and weighty connections. The feeling of the tribe was very much roused against Utu, for Tua, the injured husband, was a popular man, and one of their best fighting chiefs, whereas Utu had never distinguished himself in any way, excepting on the present occasion, which had proved him oblivious to the obligations due to a friend and neighbour. The truant pair journeyed to other parts, and remained away until Utu, tired of his toy, and wearied of the exile, determined to go home and face the consequences. So one morning an affair of honour came off on the sands of Ruapeka Bay, at Ohinemutu. Utu, accompanied by his friend, Ana, were there on one side, and Tua, with four other principals, were there on the other side. Ana was not a principal, and was not there to fight, but the four men who were with Tua had each of them come to get satisfaction as near relations to the husband, or to the wife, for the Maoris were communistic in their customs. Any of these principals could have taken Tua's children from him, and they were equally entitled to avenge his honour, for was it not their honour also?

Utu sat before these five adversaries on the sand, unarmed, provided only with a short stick called a karo, with which to ward off any spears thrown at him, or blows from other weapons that might be used. Had he been a slave he would not have been allowed to have even a karo, but must have defended himself with his hands and arms. Utu's karo had been well karakia-ed by the priest.

All being ready the duel began. Tua remained inactive while each of the four men who had accompanied him advanced in turn and threw a spear at Utu, who managed to karo, ward off, the four darts without hurt to himself. The rights of the four were now exhausted. The Atua having caused their attacks to fail, they could not be repeated without danger to themselves; any one of them who, contrary to all canons human and divine, should renew his attack, would be liable in himself or his family to misfortune (aitua) by sickness, accident, or otherwise. Even against a slave attack could not be renewed. These assailants had had every chance. The choice of weapons and how to use them had been theirs. They had chosen spears. The weight of the weapon and the distance at which to throw it had been at their option. Any one of them for that matter might have walked straight up to Utu as he sat and speared him on the spot at short point, had he been able, but they were too experienced to attempt it. Utu would have defended himself easily in that case. Rising at the right moment, and advancing a pace, he would have fixed his opponent's eye, and by a dexterous movement of his right hand would have seized and averted the thrust—thus to disarm an enemy to one who knew how was as simple as shaking hands with a friend.

As we have disposed of the four in theory and practice, let us return to Tua, whom we left looking on, apparently almost an indifferent spectator. The four had failed, and this seemed suddenly to rouse his feelings, for he went off into a dance wholly scornful in gesture of his friends, and somewhat defiant of his enemies, treating all to an exhibition of agility as he darted from place to place, and skill in brandishing his weapon, and riveting attention, his own the while being fixed in semi-challenge to the bunglers, and thus he gained his point of vantage, and wheeling, struck a blow that killed the unsuspecting Ana, whom nobody wished to hurt, and thus the duel ended as communistically as it had begun. I should say that Hea, a brother of Tua, being of a utilitarian disposition, had refrained from exercising his right at the encounter. The satisfaction he required was a bit of land. Utu recognised the claim, and gave him a nice little town site overlooking the lake.

MAORI COMMUNISM.

As in his private warfare, so in his general life. The Maori was a thorough communist. But through the warp of his communism woofs of chieftainship and priestcraft were woven into a texture strong enough to answer all the requirements of his simple civilization. Where communal usage did not reach the case the chief's was the executive governing power that dealt with it. Thus, communal usage might require a muru,* and it would be made accordingly by persons having the right. If a man's wife went wrong her people would muru him for not taking better care of her, this was usage; but if the chief ordered a muru it would be for reasons known to himself, presumably for the benefit of the tribe. If a man gave much trouble the chief might have him muru-ed, or he might take his wife from him. If he misconducted himself in war, the chief might strike him with his weapon. As a rule, however, these manifestations of authority were seldom needed, and very seldom exercised. The chieftainship of the tribe was an hereditary office, passing from father to son by the law of primogeniture; if the regular successor lacked the mental vigour and force of character necessary to the position, then another member of the hereditary family would be put in his place. The chief

*To muru a man was to strip him of his personal property or some of it, or communist property in which he had an interest might be muru-ed.

generally consulted advisers, or was supported by a council. In any case the chief could not run counter to the will of the tribe.

The priest performed many religious offices for the community. Questions of tapu were in his keeping. At times of sickness his aid was invoked. At births he was not absent, and at baptisms his presence was necessary. He advised the chief as to the will of the gods, and the greatest weight was attached to his utterances on such occasions. He always received fees in the form of presents. As a rule he supported the governing power. If the priest (tohunga) stood high in his profession, and was sent for from a distance to perform an important function, his fee would be commensurate to the event. He did not neglect the requirements of the humble members of the community. The widow with her small offering received his conscientious attention. Her child's illness was diagnosed and prescribed for and karakia-ed the same as for a more prosperous person. The priest's office was hereditary.

Although the chief carried himself with an air of authority, and the priest wore an appearance of superiority, each was subtly influenced by the communism of the body of which he formed a part. The former felt the pulse of the people before taking a step; the latter did not disregard their feelings and prejudices. Each lived in the same way as the people around him. Sometimes, however, a chief rose by violence or intrigue to such a commanding position among other tribes that his own tribe acquired perfect confidence in his judgment and ability, and followed him implicitly. Such men were Tuwhakairiora, the first Te Waharoa, Te Rauparaha, and Hongi Hika.

As I have said, the Maori was a communist. Excepting perhaps a patch of land he might own privately, and his weapons and ornaments, the only thing he could draw the line at, and safely say, 'This is mine,' was his wife, who, before she blended her life with his, had been from earliest youth in principle and practice also a communist of the free love kind, not that much love had been involved, only that 'through some shades of earthly feeling,' she had tripped from pleasure to pleasure, not waiting to be wooed, and shedding in lieu of the 'meek and vestal fires,' 'a glow so warm and yet so shadowy, too,' upon her associates, 'as made the very darkness there more sought after than light elsewhere.' May I be pardoned for adapting the lines of the poet to my subject, who was neither a Delilah nor a Messalina, but a simple Eve of nature, against whom in her own and people's eyes there was no law, nor fault to find—kahore e ture. But when she became a wife she rose to a higher sphere. Her animal habits changed as if by magic. Her communistic shell was cast, and she emerged an individual, a faithful Maori matron, with all the rights and obligations pertaining to her new condition.

But to return to our Maori communist. He could not even claim his own children exclusively. For his brother, if childless, might, and most likely would, come and take one of them away and adopt it, and his sister might come and take another; so also his wife's sister might assert a similar right, but they could not among them deprive him of all his children. Communism stepped in at that point and took his part, for was he not as well entitled as they to share in the offspring?

The house he lived in was called a wharepuni (living close together house). It contained but one room, in which both sexes, old and young, married and single, lived together night and day, and, according to size, it accommodated from say a dozen to four times that number of persons† Again, when he went to cultivate the soil, he did not go by himself, taking perhaps his son, or sons, as a European would. No, when he went he went with the commune. It was not his motion, but the motion of a body of people, whom the chief apparently led, while instinctively following the democratic desire. Men and women, boys and girls, all went together, as to a picnic, cheerful, happy, and contented, and it was a pleasant sight to see them ranged in rows, and digging with their ko-es (wooden Maori spades), as they rose and fell, and their limbs and bodies swayed rythmically to the working of the ko, and the chorus of an ancient hymn, invoking a blessing on the fruit of their labour. Still a large yield was not always a benefit, for it would sometimes induce friends and relations to come from a distance and eat the commune out of house and home.

In the same way our communist was quite unable to keep any new thing, especially in the way of clothing. Did he sell a pig, and get a blanket in payment, his father presently paid him a visit, and was seen returning with the blanket draped round his person, and if he sold some kits of corn for a shirt, a pair of trousers, and a hat, his cousin would come from five or six miles away and the hat would be given to him. Of course, the custom cut both ways, for when reduced in circumstances he, too, made calls upon his friends at auspicious times. But the system he lived under discouraged individual effort, and those who tried individually to better themselves under it sooner or later gave up the attempt, and it was not until the example of the early settlers had fully influenced another generation, stimulating it to further action, and the Native Lands Court had individualised their holdings, that the ice that bound and chilled their every effort was broken, and the communistic element in their system of civilization that had stunted enterprise and retarded material interests was greatly diminished, though not entirely removed.

But when it came to fighting, the Maori's communism helped him. When summoned to do battle for the commonwealth he instantly obeyed without conscription or recruiting, and with no swearing in, no shirking, no grumbling, he appeared at his post a trained soldier, active, willing, and determined, in an army where courts-martial were unnecessary and unknown. He was animated by a living principle, he thought not of himself, but the body he belonged to was ever in his mind. The spirit that was in him inspired the whole, giving fierceness to the war dance, zest to the tuki* of the war canoe, and proved a powerful factor in war.

Communism in war did not extend to the department of the Commander-in-Chief. The General was free to do his own thinking, and to issue his orders, and implicit obedience was rendered to him.

With certain exceptions the Maori held his land as a member of the tribe. In the matter of this, his real estate, the communistic element in his system of civilisation was well developed, and with the exception of slaves and refugees there was not a landless person in the community. As time advanced, and posterity increased, lands that had belonged to one passed into the possession of many persons, for after

*To tuki was to give the time to rowers in a canoe. To tuki to a war canoe required tact and skill. The chiefs prided themselves upon the proper performance of this function. Passing to and fro upon the narrow thwarts between the rows of rowers (itself an acrobatic feat), the kai-tuki gave the time and inspired the crew by words, exclamations, short speeches, snatches of song, all delivered to time, with gesture, attitude, and motions of his weapon, also in time. In very large canoes there were sometimes two kai-tukis, the senior of whom promenaded the after part of the vessel, while the other occupied the fore part.

several generations there would be a hapu, where one man had settled. This tendency was counteracted on the other hand by acts of individualisation within the tribal fresh boundaries, and sales of land for valuable consideration by one individual to another were by no means unknown. The subject of ancient land tenure amongst the Maoris is interesting and instructive, and would in itself fill a small volume, if treated exhaustively. Their claims were often singularly complex, and very far-reaching. Thus Ngaiterangi, in the early days, claimed and obtained payment for Tawhitirahi pa when a European bought the land about there, and this notwithstanding they had not ventured to occupy it for three hundred years, and the natives living near the place approved of the transaction ; but not until they had, in justice to themselves, already taken care to be paid for the full value of the land.

A slave was the property of the person who captured him in war. A master could kill his slave. A husband could beat his wife. A man might have more than one wife. The women worked more than the men, and had to do the more laborious work, such as carrying heavy burdens, which the men never did, for they had tapued their backs. When Christianity diminished the power of the priests, they did not strive against the innovation. Many of them became converted, and the others appeared to accept without question the change in the mind of the commune.

TUWHAKAIRIORA TRIBE.

This is a section of Ngatiporou tribe whose country extends from a point a little south of the East Cape to Potikorua, west of Point Lottin a few miles. From these points their boundaries running inland converge rapidly towards each other until they meet. Their territory, therefore, is triangular in form. We have seen how this country was occupied by the aborigines, and how Ngaetuari came from Whangara and conquered and settled upon the greater portion of it, and it will be remembered that the Ngaetuari were Hawaikians of Takitumu canoe.

About sixty years after the Ngaetuari had settled themselves, Tuwhakairiora appeared on the scene and altered the face of affairs in that district to such an extent that the tribe living there now owes its origin to him, and bears his name. Tuwhakairiora was also of Takitumu extraction, and it is of the rather remarkable Takitumuan movement that was made under him that I would tell. But first I will briefly outline the Takitumuan prelude to our story from the landing at Whangara to the time of our hero.

We have seen that Paikea, the captain of Takitumu, settled the immigrants at Whangara, after which he sailed for Hawaiki in another canoe, and so disappears from our view. About one hundred and twenty years after Paikea's time, the chiefs of the colony at Whangara were the brothers Pororangi and Tahu. The latter went south to Kaikoura, but Pororangi, from whom the Ngatiporou are named, lived and died at Whangara.

When Pororangi died, Tahu returned from Kaikoura to mourn for him, bringing a number of slaves with him. He married his brother's widow, and the issue of the union was Ruanuku, a son, to whom Tahu gave the party of slaves ; which party became a tribe, bearing the name of Ruanuku, their master. After some years, Tahu returned to the other island, taking his son with him, and thus these two are removed from the scene ; but the Ngatiruanuku were left behind to play an important part in it.

Pororangi had two sons, Hau and Ue. The latter took the country southward from Turanga. The former and his descendants went northward, settling from time to time in various places, nor stopped until they had claimed the land as far as Taumata Apanui, near Torere. Here, however, their tide of success was met and rolled back by the Whanau Apanui, a tribe of Hawaiki-Awa descent. About two hundred and seventy years after the colony had been planted at Whangara, Poromata, a descendant of Hau, took an active part in the movement northward, and settled at Whareponga, where Ngatiruanuku, who had become a numerous tribe, had arrived before him, and here they all lived for a time, beside the aboriginal Uepohatu tribe, of whom I have already made mention.

Now, Poromata was not a young man. He had several grown-up sons and daughters, who, like himself, were of a tyrannical disposition. They despised and oppressed the Ngatiruanuku as if they had been the slaves brought from Kaikoura one hundred and fifty years before ; and, ignoring the fact that they were but a few individuals surrounded by a numerous people, they plundered the best of everything the Ngatiruanuku produced, and forcibly took their women from them, and they were particularly fond of seizing the best fish from the Ruanuku canoes when they returned from fishing out at sea. At length Ngatiruanuku, goaded beyond endurance, conspired to slay the old man and his sons, and they, by surprise, attacked them while fishing, and killed them all except one son, who escaped, and nothing more is heard of him in this story.

At this time Haukotore, a brother of Poromata, lived near by at Matakukai,

He was related to Ngatiruannuku by marriage, and was on better terms with them than his brother had been. He did not attempt to avenge the death of his brother, or seek assistance for that purpose; neither did he retire from among his brother's murderers. His behaviour was altogether pusillanimous, as for many years he remained on sufferance in the presence of his natural foes, even after they had refused his request to be permitted to establish a tapu where his brother had been killed.

Very different was the spirit that animated Atakura, the youngest of Poromata's daughters. She was at Whareponga when her father and brothers were killed, and was spared by Ngatiruannuku. Her anger, however, was not appeased by their forbearance. All the thirst for revenge that was lacking in her soulless uncle was, as it were, added to her own thirst, and concentrated in her burning breast. She left Whareponga immediately, and went to Uawa, where she married for the avowed purpose of raising up a son to avenge the murder. Thence she and her husband, whose name was Ngatihau, went to Opotiki, to which place he belonged, and there a son was born whom they named Tuwhakairiora, from the odd circumstance that an uncle of his at Waiapu had lately been buried alive (or rather put in a trough made for the purpose, and placed up in a tree, for that was a mode of sepulture). From his birth Tuwhakairiora was consecrated to the office of an avenger of blood. Atakura and her husband lived at Opotiki many years, and had a family of several children. It was there that Tuwhakairiora received the education necessary to a chief, and the military training that should fit him for the part he was destined to perform. He was not like other young chiefs, for all knew, and he knew, that he had a mission to which he had been dedicated from the womb, and it was proverbial how his lusty embryonic struggles had been welcomed by his mother as a token of manhood and power to slay her father's murderers.

Thus it was that our young chief, when he came to man's estate, was the centre to whom a wide circle of adventurous spirits looked and longed for warlike excitement. Nor did he fail to take advantage of this feeling, by visiting from tribe to tribe and increasing his prestige and popularity. At length he determined to take action. For this purpose he moved with his parents to Te Kaha, Oreti, and Whangaparaoa, living at each place awhile, ingratiating themselves with the inhabitants, and drawing recruits to their cause. From the place last named his parents passed on to Kawakawa, leaving the rest of the party at Whangaparaoa, where Kahupakari, Atakura's first cousin, received them joyfully and gave her several hundred acres of land to live on. Kahupakari's father had taken part in the Ngaetuere conquest sixty years before.

Shortly after this, Tuwhakairiora followed his parents to Kawakawa, travelling by himself. On this journey he saw Ruataupare for the first time, and married her at Wharekahika in the masterful manner already described. She was the daughter of the principal chief of that district, which was peopled at that time by aboriginal tribes. Our hero required something then to soothe his feelings, for he had just hurried away through wounded pride from Whangaparaoa, where he had met his match in a young woman of rank named Hinerupe, towards whom he had conducted himself in a plantation where they were working with a freedom so unbecoming that she met him with her wooden spade, and hit him a blow on the jaw that sent him off. The plantation is called Kauae (jaw) to this day.

From Kawakawa Tuwhakairiora made an excursion to the East Cape, whence for the first time he viewed the Ngatiruannuku country, and doubtless thought upon his mission and revolved in his mind the task before him. But he was not to get vengeance yet, nor indeed for many years. Although he knew it not, he was even then in a path that would lead to a train of events fated to alter his position, and change him from a wayfaring adventurer to the warlike head of a powerful tribe. He turned and retraced his steps. He was alone, and his dog followed him. Passing near Hekawa pa, two men, Wahia and Whata, appeared and killed his dog. He slew them both, then, putting his dead dog on his back, he went on his way; but was presently overtaken by a number of men from Hekawa. He turned and killed Pito, the foremost, but others pressed on, and after slaying several he took refuge on a mound that is an island at high water. The people of Hekawa surrounded the little mound and kept him there. In this position he was seen by his younger brother, Hukarere, and recognised by his red dogskin mat. His brother, who was fishing in a canoe, came instantly to the rescue. Tuwhakairiora descended the hill, cut his way through his enemies, killing Waipao, and escaped to the canoe. That place is still called Waipao. Thus Hukarere saved his brother's life, and thus Tuwhakairiora became incensed against the Ngaetuere, and he determined to make war upon them. He sent, therefore, to his followers to muster and come to him, and they quickly responded, especially at Opotiki, where he was so well known and admired. It was with these troops that he conquered the Ngaetuere.

Now we have seen that Ngaetuere were a tribe of Takitumu descent who, sixty years before, had driven out the aboriginal Ngaoko, who were of Toi extraction. More than thirty years before that time the Ngaoko had emerged from the mountain forest of Tututohara and destroyed the aboriginal tribe named Ruawaipu, that occupied the coast from Pukeamaru to Maraehara, and killed their chief, whose name was Tamatea Arahia. Tamatea Upoko, the daughter of this chief, escaped with other refugees to Whangara, where Ngatiporou, of Takitumu, received and sheltered them. Tamatea Upoko married Uekaihau, of Ngatiporou, and in due course three sons of that marriage, Uetaha, Tamokoro and Tahania, grew up. The Ruawaipu element had, meanwhile, so strengthened itself among the Ngatiporou, that the three brothers named were able to raise an army of Ngatiporou and half-caste Ruawaipu-Ngatiporou sufficiently numerous to justify them in attacking Ngaoko, for the purpose of revenge and to regain the lost territory.

They set out, and on their march were attacked at Uawa (Tologa Bay) by Te Aetanga Hauiti, who failed to bar their passage. Again at Tawhiti mountain they were attacked by the Wahineiti, and again they forced their way against those who would have stopped them. After this they marched unmolested through the Waiapu country, belonging to the Wahineiti*, an aboriginal tribe who were a section of Te Iwi Pohatu a Maui. Having passed the East Cape the army, whom from this time I shall speak of as Ngaetuere, travelled through Horoera and Hekawa without meeting a soul, the Ngaoko had evidently fallen back to some vantage ground to await their attack. When they arrived at Kawakawa, they found the Ngaoko posted in two pas, one at Karakatuwhero, the other, Tihi o Manono, at Kopuaponamu, was the largest pa they had. A scouting party of the invaders fell in with a similar party of the people of the place, and cut them off, killing the chief, Tuteurnao. Then the Ngaoko came out of their pas in full force and attacked Ngaetuere in the open field, when the latter, by a stratagem, led Ngaoko into Awatere Gorge, and, getting them at a disadvantage, inflicted severe loss upon them, and killed their chief, Tangikaroro. At the next engagement Ngaoko were again defeated, and another chief named Rakaimokonui fell. At the third battle Ngaoko were com-

pletely worsted, and fled for the first time before their enemies. On this occasion the chiefs Maonoho and Te Awhenga were slain. On the same day the great pa Tihi o Manono was taken by assault. Ngaoko rallied, however, at the pa at Karakatuwhero, and finally at Tarapahure, another pa at Pukeamaru, but the three brothers pursued them and took these pas also, and this completed the conquest of the tribe and country. The remnant of the Ngaoko became slaves called Ngatirakaimaatapu; but they intermarried with the conquerers, and became absorbed by them.

This, then, was the tribe of Ngaetuere, against whom Tuwhakairiora was about to declare war. After a lapse of sixty years, the component parts of the tribe had consolidated into a homogeneous whole, of which the elements were probably half aboriginal and half immigrant in character. And the force, chiefly Whakatohea, that was coming against them, and destined to overthrow and absorb them—what was it? We have already seen that the people it was drawn from were a tribe of aborigines with but a strain of immigrant blood in its veins, and this is the material, united and cemented together by time, of which the Tuwhakairiora tribe is formed. From that time, more than three hundred years ago, the tribe has always been ruled by chiefs of the same distinguished Ngatiporou family.

Tuwhakairiora crossed the Awatere with his forces, and engaged and utterly defeated the Ngaetuere at Hekawa. Then he established himself at Kawakawa, and built a pa called Okanwharetoa at Awatere. Some of the Ngaetuere were now subject to him, but others were not. About this time some Ngaetumoana people killed Te Rangihekeiho of Ngaetuiti, of which tribe was Ruataupare, Tuwhakairiora's wife; this was a sufficient excuse for Tuwhakairiora to wage war against them. He fought them at the battle of Whanakaimaro, at Matakawa, and destroyed the tribe, driving the remnant off westward towards Whangaparaoa. Thus one tribe of aborigines disappeared from the district. Then another tribe of aborigines became uneasy at the presence of the invaders, and insulted them. These were the Pararake. War followed, and the battle of Pipiwhakau was fought, where the aboriginal chief Whakapuru te Rangi was slain, and his tribe was defeated and driven to Whangaparaoa. The aboriginal Ngaetuiti were allowed to remain intact because the conqueror had married into their tribe when he came from Opotiki, but they fell into a very subordinate position; nevertheless, at their desire some of the Pararake were allowed to remain in the district.

It happened that while Tuwhakairiora

---

*The Wahineiti of Waiapu are not to be confounded with the Wahineiti of Waipiro. The latter was a small tribe of Pororangi origin. The former was a section of the aborigines.

was taking a wife to himself at Whare-kahika, his brother Hukarere was similarly engaged at Whangaparaoa. He married Hinerupe, who had used her spade so well, the granddaughter of Tamakoro, one of the three brothers who led Ngaetuere from Whangara against Ngaoko. At the time of the marriage Uetaha, her father, was the chief of a large section of Ngaetuere. This alliance favoured the designs of Tu-whakairiora by neutralising at the time of active hostilities a great number of the Ngaetuere. It enabled him to conquer the tribe in detail, instead of having them all against him at one time. Not that Tuwhakairiora acted treacherously towards the Tamakoro section of Ngaetuiti. The trouble that came they brought upon them selves. The half brothers of Hinerupe were jealous of some advantages granted to her by Tuwhakairiora, who was her brother-in-law, and they cursed her; this, of course, could not be overlooked, and action was determined upon. Tuwhakairi-ora sent to friends he had made at Waiapu and Uawa, asking them to come and assist him in the forthcoming struggle, and in response the chiefs Umuariki and Kauta-harua appeared, with their respective fol-lowings. In this manner a considerable force was collected, and the campaign of Waihakia took place, resulting in the entire defeat of the Tamakoro party, whom the conqueror reduced to a state, not exactly of slavery, but of great degrada-tion.

I have now told how the tribe of Tu-whakairiora was planted and grew up on the soil where it flourishes at the present time. The war had commenced with an attack made upon Tuwhakairiora while he was visiting his cousin Kahupakiri at Kawakawa. The descendants of the people who made that attack are now in-corporated in the general tribe of Tuwhaka-iriora, under the name of Te Wakeoneone.

Many years had elapsed before these conquests were all completed, and affairs connected with them consolidated suf-ficiently to permit Tuwhakairiora to turn his hand to that to which he had been ordained. At length, however, a time arrived when he felt able to discharge the duty imposed, and preparations were ac-cordingly made to assemble a force to chastise the murderers of his grandfather. From Opotiki, where he was so popular, he easily obtained as many men as he wanted. With these added to his own troops, he set sail in a fleet of canoes for the country of Ngatiruanuku, where one morning before daybreak he surprised and carried by assault Tonganiu, a pa, and killed Kahu-tapu, the chief of that place. Then he fought the battle of Hikutawatawa in the open, and took two other pas called Ureparaheka,

and another. Many were killed in these pas, the people who escaped fled inland, leaving all their land and property to the victors. Tuwhakairiora then considered that ample revenge had been obtained, and he returned home to Kawakawa, leaving his great uncle Haukotore and other relations, who had continued to live there after the murder, in possession of the land.

Mate, the sister of Atakura, heard at Turanga of Tuwhakairiora's campaign, and that two or three pas had fallen, and said, 'My sister's side has avenged, but mine is not avenged,' and she sent for Pakanui, her grandson, to return from a war he was prosecuting in the south, and directed him to wage war against the re-maining portion of Ngatiruanuku, and against their allies, the Wahineiti of Poro-rangi, who lived at Waipiro.

Pakanui obeyed his grandmother, and fitted out a number of canoes for an ex-pedition, and for want of warriors he manned them with a force so inadequate to the object intended, that he devised the extraordinary ruse of taking the women and children in the canoes, in order to deceive Ngatiruanuku as to the nature of the flotilla, and for the rest he hoped that some accident might befriend him. When Pakanui and his party arrived at Waipiro, they landed there and camped on the shore. To all appearance they were travellers en route, the presence of the women and children quite put the people there off their guard; but the strangers could not remain indefinitely, their chief knew this, and was puzzled what action next to take. He could not send for Tuwhakairi-ora's assistance, for his enterprise was a sort of set off against what that chief had done. He could not attack the enemy openly without courting defeat, while to return home would be to make himself a laughing stock, and nothing had happened, or was likely to happen, to assist him. In this dilemma he racked his brains, and an idea occurred to him, upon which, for want of a better, he determined to act. He told each man to make a hand net, such as was used for catching small fish among the rocks on the seashore; with the help of the women this task was soon accomplished. Then he distributed his men along the shore in open order a little before the right time of tide for fishing, and they were all engaged in fishing at the many little channels in the rocks through which the tide flowed, some of them made artificially, and each belonging to some man in the neighbouring pa.*

'In many parts of the East Coast, south of Hicks' Bay, a limestone formation prevails, the strata of which, tilted at a high angle, run in parallel lines from the land to the sea. At the

The owners of these fishing channels did not admire the freedom of the strangers with their private fishing ground, and they mustered to occupy their fishing channels, and at the right time of tide they presented themselves in a body, each man with his hand net, and their chief Rangirakaikura at their head. The chief found that Pakanui had appropriated his stream, for Paka had noted beforehand which was the chief's stream, and said to him, 'And where am I to fish?' Paka promptly drew his net out of the water, and replied, 'Fish here,' and he stood beside Rangi as he fished. This little pantomime was enacted all along the line, until Pakanui saw all his men distributed like Thugs, each man standing close to a man of the other side, apparently looking at the fishing, really awaiting the pre-arranged signal that he was to make, the tide meanwhile washing high over their feet. Suddenly the signal was given, then each man of Paka's side simultaneously drew a mere, attached to his foot under water, and throwing his net over the head of his enemy entangled him in it, while he killed him with the mere. In this manner Pakanui's party killed one hundred fighting men, including the chief, and struck such a terror into the remainder of the enemy, that Pakanui was able to follow up the success effectively. This affair is known as Te Ika Koraparua, which may be freely rendered, 'Two fish in one net.' The kehe and the man. It took place near Tangitu stream, between Akuaku and Whareponga. The Ngatirnanuku fled inland, whither they were followed and finally destroyed. Thus Mate was avenged for the death of Poromata, her father, by the extinction of the remnant of Ruanuku people whom Tuwhakairiora had spared, but the Wahineiti tribe remained in full force south of Waipiro stream, being too numerous for Pakanui to venture to disturb them. However, he settled on the land he had conquered, and lived there several years, at the end of which he was compelled by the hostility of the Wahineiti to obtain the aid of Tuwhakairiora, who came with a strong force and crushed the Wahineiti at the battle of Rorohukatai, fought on Waipiro beach (so named because the brains of men were mingled there with the froth of the tide), and by taking their three pas, Poroporo, Turangamoahu and Maungakowhai. At the end of the war Tuwhakairiora returned home, whence he sent Iritekura, his

niece, to occupy the conquered territory. She went with her family to Waipiro about three hundred and thirty years ago. She lived and died there, and her descendants, who bear her name, live there at the present time.

But Iritekura, who founded the tribe of that name, is not the only Maori woman whose name figures in the history of her race.

It was a woman, Torere, who swam ashore from Tainui canoe, and founded the Ngaitai tribe.

It was the woman, Muriwai, who led the Ngatiawa to Whakatane in Mataatua canoe.

It was a woman, Atakura, that caused several pas to be destroyed out of revenge.

It was a woman, Mate, that caused a tribe to be annihilated from feelings of revenge.

It was a woman, Hinewaha, whose thirst for revenge enabled her to raise the Ngatitematera at the Thames, and incite them to make war on Ngamarama at Katikati, because her brothers had been slain in battle by the latter.

It was a woman, Ruataupare, who invaded the Wahineiti at Tokomaru, and took that country from them, and founded a tribe that bears her name now.

It was a woman, Moenga, who led the Amazons at the battle of Mangatara, and routed the enemy.

But if there have been women political, women revengeful, and military women, amongst the Maoris, there have also been merciful women, and women of a peaceful disposition.

Of such was the woman Kuranhirangi, who intervened on the field of battle and made peace between Te Roroterangi and Ngaeterangi at Maketu, and terminated a war that had lasted many years, and had probably cost thousands of lives, for great efforts had been made by many tribes to recover that place from Ngaeterangi.

When Te Rohu, a chief of Hauraki, influenced by revenge, took the large pa at Tauranga called Te Papa, and slew its unfortunate people, it was a woman, one of his wives (whose name I regret I have mislaid), who persuaded him to relinquish his intention to destroy Otumoetai, and to be satisfied with the utu obtained. She saved the lives in that large pa of, perhaps two thousand persons, and returned home with her husband.

Now, observe the sequel. It happened within a short time after, that Te Waharoa urged Ngaeterangi to help him in the approaching campaign against the Hauraki tribes at Haowhenua. They responded to the call, and sent a contingent of about two hundred men, who all returned home without fighting because they had received a message from that woman before the battle of Taumatawiwi asking if they remembered Otumoetai?*

Lastly, it was a woman, Mapihiterangi, who stopped the chronic state of warfare between Ngaeterangi and the remnant of Ngatiranginui. She was a Ngaeterangi woman of rank, who, unknown to her own tribe, passed over to the enemy's tribe, and married its guerilla chief.

And it was quite a common thing in ancient Maori life and history, for women of rank to sacrifice their own feelings, and all they held dear, and marry stranger chiefs of other tribes, from whom in times of public emergency assistance was required.

'The return home of Ngaeterangi without fighting at Taumatawiwi, is not mentioned in the story of Te Waharoa. I had heard of that return at the time I wrote that book, from a man who was a slave in the Haowhenua pa. All he could say was that Ngaeterangi had turned back at Horotiu River, without crossing it, and therefore, without reaching the field of Taumatawiwi. I hesitated, however, to attach historical weight to an improbable and inexplicable story. I have since learned from Ngaeterangi chiefs now deceased, that the story of the slave was correct, and that the woman's message was the cause of the extraordinary proceeding.